CRE▲TIVE
HOMEOWNER®

can't fail window
treatments

COPYRIGHT © 2009

CRE**A**TIVE
HOMEOWNER®

A Division of Federal Marketing Corp.
Upper Saddle River, NJ

CAN'T FAIL WINDOW TREATMENTS

SENIOR EDITOR Kathie Robitz
GRAPHIC DESIGNER Kathryn Wityk
PHOTO COORDINATOR Mary Dolan
DIGITAL IMAGING SPECIALIST Frank Dyer
EDITORIAL ASSISTANT Sara Markowitz
INDEXER Schroeder Indexing Services
FRONT AND BACK COVER PHOTOGRAPHY Melabee M Miller

CREATIVE HOMEOWNER

VICE PRESIDENT AND PUBLISHER Timothy O. Bakke
MANAGING EDITOR Fran J. Donegan
ART DIRECTOR David Geer
PRODUCTION COORDINATOR Sara M. Markowitz

Current Printing (last digit)
10 9 8 7 6 5 4 3 2 1

Can't Fail Window Treatments, First Edition
Library of Congress Control Number: 2008934549
ISBN-10: 1-58011-451-2
ISBN-13: 978-1-58011-451-6

CREATIVE HOMEOWNER®
A Division of Federal Marketing Corp.
24 Park Way
Upper Saddle River, NJ 07458
www.creativehomeowner.com

dedication

I would like to dedicate this book to my wonderful husband and family
for their unending love and support.

acknowledgments

I want to thank Melabee M Miller for being such a great photographer
and so much fun to work with to boot! Also a huge thank you to
Kathie Robitz and her team, including designer Kathryn Wityk,
for the endless hours put in to make this book a reality. And finally,
thanks to my clients for allowing me to interpret their dreams and
express my inspirations in wonderful window treatments.

contents

introduction

What a difference the right window treatment can make! The trick is to choose the one that will address your needs, whether you want to add style, control light and air, create screening from the outdoors, or even visually correct awkward window sizes, shapes, or locations. *Can't Fail Window Treatments* provides ideas for addressing all of these issues. You'll find this book easy to navigate, too. Information and photos are grouped by window-treatment types—draperies, swags, pelmets and valances, blinds and shades, shutters and screens, and sheers—as well as accessories, including trimmings and hardware. A separate section is entirely devoted to problem solving. You'll find recommendations for treating windows of different sizes, unusual configurations and shapes, corner windows, and more.

So whatever you do, don't skip the window treatments when you are decorating or redecorating. If you're unsure of how to handle them, let this book be your guide. You can't fail!

Part 1

from plain to
personality
plus

SWAGS &
TAILS IN
EMBROIDERED
SILK

from plain to personality plus

why window treatments are important

Style, privacy, and light control—
the right window treatment can provide
any or all of these.

A window treatment is to a window what a frame is to a painting. Framing a window in beautiful fabric accentuates the opening, defining its relationship to the room as a whole. When they are dressed properly, windows can be commanding—outlining a beautiful view or making a design or architectural statement—or simply functional—a means for controlling light and air, as well as protection from prying eyes.

Whether the window in question is the focal point or simply a side note in a room, it will need some kind of treatment. In most cases, in fact, an undressed window looks unfinished. Yet on occasion, even I must admit that some windows may be better left unadorned— either the view or the window itself is so pleasing that a window treatment would be a distraction. Some windows are simply beautiful architectural features.

For now, take a look at the different window treatments on the following pages and note the important role they have played in the overall design and function of each room.

Control Privacy Stylishly

Earth colors give this master bedroom a calm feeling. The full **drapes are dressed asymmetrically** for just a touch of drama. A **roller shade,** concealed behind the drapes, enables the client to have **privacy and control light** without fussing with the panels.

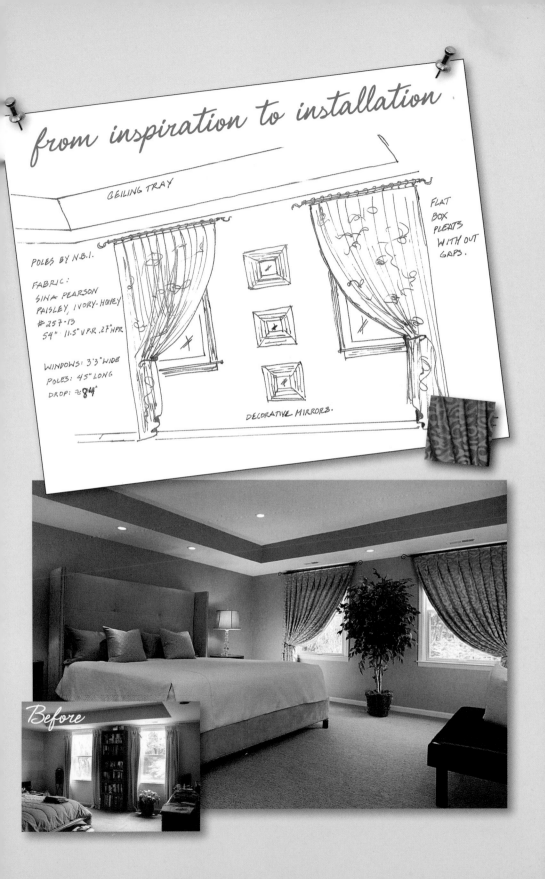

from inspiration to installation

CEILING TRAY

POLES BY N.B.I.

FABRIC:
SINA PEARSON
PAISLEY, IVORY-HONEY
#257-13
54" 11.5" V.P.R .27" H.P.R

WINDOWS: 3'3" WIDE
POLES: 45" LONG
DROP: ≈ 84"

FLAT
BOX
PLEATS
WITH OUT
GAPS.

DECORATIVE MIRRORS.

Before

Add Femininity to a Bedroom

The soft teal color, above, and the pretty treatment are **femininity personified!** The drapery rod curves forward, giving extra depth to the window. **Custom details,** including **goblet pleats, beaded trim** along the leading edge, **ribbon tassel tiebacks,** and a **fabric roller blind** with a rouched-fabric band and more beaded trim make the room soft and inviting.

Protect Furnishings from Fading

The drapes in this room, opposite, held back with **tasseled tiebacks,** have been paired with a Roman blind that is **lined with blackout fabric** for strong light control. I used a **pinstripe fabric** reminiscent of men's shirting to make this room a little less formal looking. The **tailored valance** is somewhat whimsical with contrast triangles in green and **accent buttons** in blue.

Before

Balance a Room's Colors and Patterns

For the very traditional dining room opposite, I selected a **classic floral-patterned fabric** to offset the dark-red damask wallpaper. The drapes are mounted on a **curved rod** with **goblet pleats** that have a **contrast button** for an accent at the base of each one. **Tassel fringe** highlights the leading edge, and the drapes are secured with a **decorative rosette.** Placing the holdback below the halfway point of the drapes increases the swag, adding **extra drama** to the formal look.

Emphasize a Theme

The garden room below has green painted cabinets and floral wallpaper, so the choice of another **floral for the window treatments** was obvious, considering the use of the space. A **rust-color contrast band** at the top of the **box-pleated valance** separates the two patterns while picking up a color found in both prints.

why window treatments are important

Underscore the Interior Design

The **height of formality** is achieved by combining a **classic striped silk** with a strictly traditional style, above. **Cream and gold silk swags and jabots** with dress drapes are trimmed with an **elegant silk fringe.** The swags are draped on **two-tone painted poles and finials** that complement the gold and cream color scheme. **Sheer curtains** finish the look while providing **sun protection** for the rug and furniture.

Frame a Garden View

Cream embroidered-silk fabric provides a **sharp contrast** against the oxblood-color walls of the formal dining room opposite. **Formal swags and jabots** frame the bay window, **highlighting the view** and permitting natural light to enter unobstructed. The silk fabric picks up all the colors in the rug to create a **warm and dramatic color palette.**

from inspiration to installation

SWAGS &
TAILS IN
EMBROIDERED
SILK

Before

Perk Up Understated Furnishings

The **red-tone ikat-printed fabric** above adds the visual punch needed in this neutral family room. Simple **wrought-iron poles and finials** provide just a minimal flourish so as not to compete with the fabric.

Add Grandeur to Plain Windows

The **black pom-pom trim** adds a defining line to the curvilinear shape of the valances, below. Note how the maximum amount of window is exposed by **placing the valance high** and the drapes wide; just the window trim is covered. Doing this creates an **illusion of greater height and width.**

why window treatments are important

details

The pom-pom fringe at left defines the fun shape of the bell and swag valance. A fabric rosette tops the pleats. The devil is in the details!

Maintain a Mood
Cream-color textured silk was used to **"keep the drapes quiet"** in the living room at right and below, which has been painted a lovely shade of café-au-lait. A **curved, pinch-pleated valance,** dressed with a **ribbon-style tassel fringe,** completely frames the view of a country-side setting. **Matching tiebacks** hold back the dress panels.

details

Note that the valance's pleats, left, are full height and topped with a contrast cord. (Some box-pleated treatments have a flat band along the top that shortens the pleats. In that case, they are typically finished with a contrast cord at the top and bottom edge of the flat band.)

Bring the Outdoors Inside

The casual living room's **bold plaid window treatment,** below, features a **box-pleated valance.** Its shape echoes the curve of the window, while the **panels flank the window seat** to frame the garden view.

Add Visual Interest with Texture

This family room is all about texture—from the brick fireplace to the mottled wallpaper to the plush chenille sofa. A plain, woven fabric was selected for the valance so that it does not compete with the texture of the grass-cloth blinds. Whimsical, decorative monkey brackets enhance the African theme established with the homeowner's collection of safari artifacts.

why window treatments are important

Complement Great Architecture

A **large bay window,** opposite, in a formal townhouse commanded a window treatment with "presence." There are three layers to this one: **formal swags and jabots with floor-length dress drapes, sill-length draw drapes,** and **operable fabric blinds.** So although the look is elaborate, a simple roller shade controls the light and privacy.

Improve the Appearance of Small Windows

Shaped, upholstered lambrequins frame the small windows in a basement family breakfast room, above. **Black brush fringe** dramatically outlines the curvilinear shape of the lambrequin. The **toile fabric** continues the overall pattern of the **matching wallpaper,** creating a strong statement of **pattern on pattern** in the room.

making a statement

Window treatments are a fantastic way to create design impact.

Dressing a window is a great way to express your style. Depending on the architecture and purpose of the room, the window treatments can be whimsical or practical, dramatic or subtle, ornate or basic. Window treatments may also provide an opportunity to unify the palette when there are several colors in a room, update the existing decor, or create a focal point. The range of fabrics, materials, and styles is vast, from silk to linen, woven textures to floral prints, and bold patterns to subdued neutrals. There is a color, texture, and style for every taste.

Cozy Up with Color

Rich russet drapery panels bring additional **seasonal hues** into the room, left. This **versatile** treatment features rings at the top that make it **easy to move** the panels across the rod.

Capture a Mood

In the richly appointed paneled library, opposite, the mood of an intimate English clubroom is enhanced by **floor-length dress drapes** and **shaped upholstered pelmets** done in a **traditional floral linen fabric**. Cord trims add detail and give a crisp line to the leading edge of the fabric.

making a statement

Special Finishing Details Add Richness

The custom-made gray silk **swag and jabot treatment,** opposite, has a **center bell feature** that is **dressed with fringe** and **accented with a tassel.** The soothing gray with the taupe color of the trim maintains an elegant look for this formal room.

Fabric Counterbalances Hard Materials

For a family bath, above, that is all about stone and tile, earth tones, and textures, a single **asymmetrical rust-color toile drape** (as seen reflected in the mirror) introduces just the right touch of color and softness. The **wrought-iron finial and holdback hardware** coordinate well with the **oil-rubbed bronze fittings.**

details

A degree of clarity and crispness is provided with a border of black velvet on a black-and-white toile fabric.

Compose a "Picture"

This straight **box-pleated valance** with a **contrast bound-edge** beautifully frames both the window and the furniture. The width of the pleat allows the pattern repeat to be seen clearly while the gathered drapes bunch the pattern together. The **dark barley-twist pole and finial** provide additional decoration.

A Big Little Flourish

A **gathered ruffle valance** placed below the top of the window **adds a touch of color and whimsy** to this garden room. It's a perfect example of "less is more." If this window had no window treatment, it would simply look unfinished.

making a statement

Pattern Perks Up a Solid-Color Scheme

A large pattern on the fabric, right, brings the interest that's needed to **enliven neutral walls** and solid-tone furniture. The print picks up the colors of the paint and the sofa perfectly to keep the overall look of the room cohesive.

Updating a Classic

Although typically considered a traditional style, the swag, above, is dressed casually with **asymmetrical end drapes** for a more modern look. The strong contrast between the dark walls and the white drapes and white shutters makes a **clean, contemporary statement**. Such **strong contrasting colors appear bold and dramatic.**

making a statement

details

A full brush fringe provides a nice detail along the leading edge of the drape here. Fringes are typically opulent and always add a rich touch to curtains. They are especially appropriate in period-style rooms.

Dramatic and Private

The fullness of the drapes below makes the room feel **cocoonlike**. Again, **the pattern in the fabric pulls together the colors** of the solid walls and furniture, which enhances the feeling of almost complete enclosure. The details of fringe down the leading edge and holdbacks add interest and **a hint of luxury.**

Opulent Effects

In the case of the room opposite, high ceilings allow for lots of fabric to drape behind a high holdback, creating the **illusion of "Italian stringing"**—a method of stringing along the back of the drape in a manner similar to a Roman blind. In this case, however, the strings are positioned on a 45-deg. angle to pull the drape up into a fixed gather for an **ultra-luxurious effect. Goblet pleats** with a **contrast lining** are the types of additional detail that distinguish these dressed windows.

from inspiration to installation

SHEERS &
TIEBACKS

LIVING
ROOM

FABRIC:
STRIPED SILK
OLD WORLD
WEAVERS
BEU0222
GARVYN
COLOR
BL002
CHAMPAGNE
54"

PR: 4' V
13' 4" H

PLEATED
SWAGS
W/GOBLET
& BELL @
ENDS

DRESS (TO
DRAPES (BREAK
         ON
         FLOOR)
W/A SHEER
ROMAN
BLIND *
BELOW

* USE LT. WT. PLEXI RODS
TO FORM CURVE IN
ROMAN BLIND

Before

Perfect Compromise

Here is a look with clean lines, yet it's still on the formal side.
Because the client wanted privacy and didn't care for floor-length
sheers, I added a soft-fold, sheer-fabric Roman shade.

details

This modified swag treatment is enhanced with the use of a striped silk fabric. The soft colors do not compete with the strong palette of the chairs because similar tones can be found in the upholstery fabric's print.

Add Over-the-Top Punch to a Period Room

Take a **simple fabric;** use lots of it; **trim it with fringe;** dress it dramatically by pinning it up to reveal a **contrast lining;** top it all off with **decorative rosettes and cord**. That's the recipe for a real **show stopper!** Here, the color, the treatment, and the pattern all work together to create an amazing look for a **great Victorian room.**

making a statement

Adding Yin to Yang

The walls of this beautifully paneled front hall embody **classic tradition.** But to make it a bit more feminine, the window is dressed with a **floral linen,** inside-mounted curtain with **goblet pleats and silk tassel fringe.** I used a subtle hint of another color, lavender, with a **sheer soft-fold Roman blind.**

form follows function

Consider air and light, the view, and your privacy when you choose a window treatment.

You can use a window treatment to add style to a room, but it can be practical as well as decorative. In fact, historically, the function of heavy curtains and drapes was to insulate a room against cold air. Curtains were also used as a way to create privacy or a partition where none existed.

Today, window treatments are still serviceable. Drapes can be closed for privacy at night; or you can fling them open to flood a room with early morning sunlight. Blinds, too, can provide light control as well as insulation. Slatted blinds are adjustable, allowing you to prevent glare, control air, or create dramatic bands of sunlight across a room. The varying opacity of fabric blinds offers more—or less—light control. Fabric blinds or shades also have insulating qualities. Combining an interlining fabric with a standard lining adds a temperature cushion, blocking the cold air between the drape and the window. This type of window treatment will also serve as a noise buffer—a great solution for urban dwellers attempting to escape the din of the city. From sunlight to sound, window treatments can offer a solution and a level of control to suit your home and your needs.

A Shaded View

Today's windows are often **better insulated,** but they may still require covering for privacy. In this master bath, elegant **silk-embroidered dress drapes** have been paired with an **Austrian blind** trimmed in beaded fringe **that can be lowered** for privacy. As a bonus, all this fabric softens the effect of the hard surfaces of the marble and fittings.

Transforming Space

This space, above, was transformed from a plain sun porch into a formal living room that recieves generous light from a southeastern exposure. **Embroidered silk drapes** in a deep rust color are left open during the day to **allow natural light to warm the room.** At night, the panels can be closed to keep the room cozy.

Drawing Room

The drapery **panels stack neatly** into the corner, opposite, when the curtains are pulled back. **Classic pinch pleat** with **tassel fringe** is a timeless treatment.

form follows function

from inspiration to installation

DRAW DRAPES
AS PER
FRENCH
DOORS

WINDOWS: 2 6' WIDE

Added Presence

Draw drapes with a "fall-over" heading trimmed with fringe add presence to a pair of moderate-size windows. The look is casual thanks to a fabric that is a muted, ethnic print, which works well with the furnishings. The grass-cloth blind behind the drapes filters the light.

Before

form follows function

Simple Works
A simple treatment with a tab heading on sheer, unlined panels keeps this room light while maintaining privacy. The wood pole and finial, as well as the contrast-button detail, add a casual note that works well with the pine furniture.

Counterbalancing a Large Solid-Color Sofa

Floral linen fabric complements the green walls of this comfortable family room. The solid-color leather sofa called for pattern in the drapes and the **floral theme pulls in the garden from outside**. Simple dress drapes on wood poles and finials is all that is needed here for a **smart but casual look**.

form follows function

Adding a "Wow" Effect—the Easy Way

The **casual heading** of this drape creates a pattern in the striped fabric—the rings pull the fabric up and it swags down in between the rings to create a scalloped effect. A feeling of luxury is achieved with **pooling the drape on the floor.** This is a great example of a **simple yet elegant** way to make the curtains look extra special.

Quiet Mood

Two **contrasting colors create drama** at the window, opposite. The **dark-brown dress drapes** add a feeling of warmth and look great with the paneling. The **full white under-drapes** serve two purposes: they provide **privacy and light control,** while also adding a **sharp contrast in color,** completing the smart look of this comfortable library.

A Simple Solution

In this **Zen-like breakfast room,** below, a simple window treatment was needed to **soften the small windows** in the space. Using a **sheer fabric** in a London blind **allows the light to filter through** while providing a subtle graphic line at the window.

form follows function

Redefining Details

Windows as pretty as these **leaded casements** should
be seen, not covered! To keep them in view and easy to
open, they remain undressed. The **transoms,** however,
sport pretty green swags—minus tails—to draw the
eye and add color.

from inspiration to installation

SINGLE WINDOW · 3' WIDE
VALANCE 20" DROP @ ENDS
15" IN CENTER.

PINCH
PLEAT
CURVED
VALANCE
W/ TASSEL
FRINGE
ON POLES §
FINIALS BY
NBI.

BAMBOO
BLIND
BY
NBI

FABRIC: VERVAIN, CARDOMON, CINNAMON
54" W ; 2.2" P.R.
100% LINEN

FRINGE: KRAVET # TA 5203-16
CHENILLE § RIBBON TASSELS

Blind Ambition

A single window in a room did not call for a full window treatment because it is next to French doors with floor-length curtains. By keeping the valance and the grass-cloth blind simple, the overall look of the design remains unified and practical.

Before

draperies

Window treatments fall into one of two categories—soft (made of fabric) or hard. Draperies are in the first category.

The terms "drapes," "draperies," and "curtains" are often used interchangeably. In this book, I use the term "dress drapes," to refer to end panels typically made of only full- or half-widths of fabric, therefore not wide enough to close. They are probably the most popular style today. Hanging from decorative poles and finials, they create a simple but refined look. This style can be achieved with a wide range of fabrics—anything from rich, sumptuous silks to plain linens. Dress drapes are quite often paired with a secondary, operable shade in the center if privacy or light control is desired. This could be anything from a fancy Austrian shade of beaded silk to a simple cotton fabric with plain braided trim.

Draw drapes, those that can be drawn completely across a window, use more fabric—usually two and one-half times the width of the window. Similar to dress drapes in style and design, draw drapes combine function and style and are popular, as well. They can have great impact on a room, depending on the fabric. In addition, draw drapes provide excellent insulation and noise control.

Depending on the window, the effect you desire, and any practical considerations, drapes and curtains may be sill-length, below-sill length, floor-length, or trailing—also called "puddled."

details

It's always important to choose the right length for your draperies, especially when they are paired with glass doors. It should be easy to move the panels back and forth, which means avoiding puddled curtains and choosing ones that ever-so-slightly brush the floor.

from inspiration to installation

MAIN DRAPE-
RUN PLAID
STRAIGHT

PLAID VALANCES
ON DIAGONAL

FRENCH
DOORS

SAILER STRETCH CURTAINS

Dressed in Plaid

The timeless color combination of blue and tan add a calm tone to this breakfast area. Note how the plaid was set on the diagonal in the attached 'fall-over' valance to create visual contrast and interest.

Touch of Sophistication

Understated elegance is achieved with the use of a silk stripe fabric in a simple treatment. Tassel trim creates a cascade of texture down the leading edge. The colors—muted gold, green, and cream—have a touch of sophistication and combine to create a formal yet inviting space. The poles and finials pick up the gold-tone highlights in the fabric.

Fabric Finesse

The use of a **sumptuous fabric** can make all the difference in a **simple drapery design.** This **heraldic-print chenille adds texture, pattern, and color** to a subdued style. **Dark wood poles and finials** add a masculine note.

A Fine Balance

Dress drapes with **raspberry-colored brush fringe** flank a **blue flat-fold Roman shade** outlined in black, adding another accent color to this youthful room. The **poles and finials** were kept simple with a **painted white finish.** The window treatment provides the **perfect balance for the striped wallpaper and toile bedspread.** This is a room that can grow with a teenager.

Before

All Things Being Equal

A feeling of freshness sets the tone in this guest room with **windows of differing heights.** Drapes were installed at the break in the window with the transom so that they align at the top with the ones that dress the single side window. The **coral-and-white patterned drapes** have a **goblet-pleated (cup-shaped) heading** and a **solid coral-color cotton binding** that defines the edges.

Balancing Act

Here's another idea for treating windows of different sizes. In this case, the **unifying elements are the drapery fabric,** which was also used for the pelmet, and the **Roman shades.** Also, notice that the top of the pelmet **aligns with the pole.**

Understated Elegance

This **heavy woven fabric in a neutral color,** below, drapes beautifully, making an **elegant statement** on its own in this **earth-tone family room.** The drapes are installed on a **traverse rod (a track system),** so there aren't any rings. A **decorative cord** that is knotted and swagged between each pleat and a **rich blue braid** down the leading edge add a little extra oomph.

Compound Interest

A **curved rod, goblet pleats, and a contrast button** are effective ways to add lots of interest to formal drapes, opposite. The **classic floral pattern** enhances the depth of color on the walls. And the **multicolor tassel fringe down the leading edge** picks up the rest of the hues in the room.

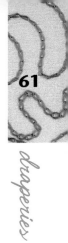

draperies

from inspiration to installation

HANG DRAPES TIGHT TO
BOTTOM OF SOFFIT

LINE OF
SOFFIT

TAN & BUTTERSCOTCH
SWIRL FABRIC

FLAT-FOLD PLEATS

DRESSED ASYMMETRICALLY

WROUGHT IRON POLE, FINIALS & HOLDBACKS

A Soft Sweep

Dressing a window asymmetrically can be quite fun. A flat box pleat on this drape creates the same amount of fullness as a standard pinch pleat, yet it is a more contemporary, clean look. Privacy and light control are achieved with a blackout roller shade that rolls up behind the drape during the day.

details

A fabric's weight is an important consideration for a drape because it affects the way the curtain will hang. This one's structured heading required a heavier fabric in order to create the smooth, regular folds.

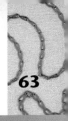

Playful Pattern

Horses and cowboys on the patterned drapes above add to the **Old West theme** of this young boy's bedroom. A **plaid banded edge on the drapes** is a smart way to provide more patterns and add interest at the same time. **Venetian blinds in wood** lend warmth and texture while easing light and privacy control.

draperies

Cosmopolitan Calm

Subtlety and elegance are established with the **rich cream fabric on these neutral drapes**, opposite. The quiet color is perfect for this transitional dining room. The **trellis-pattern sheer shade** adds to the **uptown look** of the design. This is a lovely example of how **color can have a calming effect.**

Kitchen Warmth

A **lively pattern in a simple drape adds color and warmth** to this kitchen, above. The **wrought-iron pole** does not distract from the pretty fabric. Note the **contrast band along the full height of the heading.**

Top of the Line
Shirring the fabric over the rod created a clever heading in these drapes. The gathers are held together with **a band of the same material.** These **details add an element of interest** without competing with the simplicity of the drapes.

draperies

High Drama

Because these **walls and drapes are in the same color family,** high drama is achieved with the **abundance of fabric and the contrast trim.** The **black accents** pick up the pillow and lampshade colors for a very smart look.

from inspiration to installation

DINING ROOM: DRESS DRAPES WITH TIEBACKS & SHAPED PELMET.

Corner Fit

This view illustrates how the drapes' shaped pelmet meets in the corner and how the proportion of the curve is scaled down for the smaller window.

Pretty Curves

Dress drapes, accompanied by a curved blue and tan damask-upholstered pelmet, frame a large bay window in a formal dining room. The undulating shape of the pelmet breaks up the rectilinear nature of the angular bay. Tassel tiebacks add a finishing touch.

details

Tasseled rope tiebacks arranged on hooks that have been mounted on the frames of the windows can easily be released to allow the drapes to be drawn shut when privacy is desired.

Sublime Subtlety

At first glance, these drapes look simple, but upon closer observation, the beauty of the fabric—a **contemporary neutral-color crewel** with **tone-on-tone stitches in a swirl pattern**—is revealed. These dress drapes on **wrought-iron poles with wood-tone finials** are the perfect solution for a casual family room.

draperies

Toned-Down Formality

A **tab heading** gives the drapes in this formal dining room a **slightly casual touch.** However, the **neutral palette maintains the elegant look** of the overall scheme.

The Golden Age of Dutch Art

Simple Sensation

The drapes' solid butterscotch-colored fabric provides the perfect tonal balance for this pretty living room. The fabric picks up the color in the art over the fireplace, the lamps, and the throw pillow. This room is a study in subtlety, which is hard to achieve. Over-the-top is a look that is a lot easier to create than one that is simple and beautiful.

Understated Elegance

Soft color and texture are the keys to these dress drapes with a **scalloped heading edged with a thin cord.** The **teal fabric has small embroidered leaves** and the **beige Roman blinds have an overall leaf pattern.**

draperies

A Refined Country Look

This living room is flooded with light and the **pretty pattern of the dress drapes creates a fresh backdrop.** Note how **one long pole is used for the full length** of the French door and sidelights, creating an **uninterrupted flow** for the drapes.

swags

From formal, heavily tailored designs to casual scarves, swags are versatile. Use them with or without another treatment.

Swags and jabots—also called "tails," which typically provide a classically elegant look—are often designed for use in formal or period-style interiors. However, with the right fabric and trim, they can combine form and function for a beautiful, but casual look, too.

A swag is a sweeping scallop- or crescent-shape drape of fabric at the top of a window. A jabot is the vertical element in a swag-and-jabot treatment. Swags can be symmetrically or asymmetrically dressed, trimmed with beautiful beads, or edged in a contrasting band of fabric. They can hang from a pole, or you can even mount them on a board—the photographs and sketches here can clarify the details of these different designs and terms. I have designed swags and jabots in a wide range of styles—from the finest trimmed silk for a formal dining room to leather-trimmed open weave linen for a casual powder room. The world is your oyster when it comes to personalizing the style and statement you want for your windows.

Easy Style

A **feeling of lightness** is achieved by using a **sheer fabric** for this **casual swag scarf treatment.** The fabric is simply **draped and overlapped over a pole. White shutters** offer privacy and light control and contribute to the **clean look** of this teenager's bedroom.

from inspiration to installation

DESIGNER'S GUILD
RED & WHITE FLORAL

FORMAL
SWAGS
W/TASSEL
FRINGE

RED
CONTRAST
LINED
JABOTS

RED
TASSEL
TIE-BACKS

High Fashion

This bold print manages to introduce cheerfulness and drama at the same time. The drapes, which feature a triple-swag top treatment, actually frame a pair of French doors that lead into a hallway. Taking the look almost to the ceiling, which is high, adds to the dramatic effect. (See Chapter 12, Trimmings, for a close up look of the swag and the fringe here.)

French-Country Accent

The size of this **gathered swag** is scaled down accordingly and works very well to **soften the French door** and reinforce the design theme. A **blue-and-white check with white fringe** lends itself to the **French Country-inspired kitchen** while dressing things up smartly.

Classical References

Who says a bathroom can't be as elegant as any other room? **Multilayered swags trimmed with tassels and cord** dress up the bay window in this master bath, evoking the **grandeur of ancient Rome.**

swags

from inspiration to installation

CREAM DAMASK
DRESS-MAKER SWAGS
W/NO JABOTS!

CREAM
LEAF
PATTERNED
ROMAN
BLIND

Pleasingly Precise

A dressmaker's detail, above, gives these elegant swags a unique look.

Artfully Asymmetrical

Gathered damask swags, left, dressed asymmetrically as they flank the bed, create a stunning statement in a blue-and-cream master suite. The coordinating shade can be lowered for privacy and to completely block sunlight.

Thrice as Nice

The room's largest window, above, features a triple-swag valance over dress drapes.
The Roman blinds have been made in a complementary fabric with a slight texture.

Elegant Edging

A **thick teal ribbon-cord** edges both the drapes and the teal swags, right, while the **gold swags are unadorned.**

Alternate Hues

Two colors are used for these **formal swags and jabot valances** in a blue toned dining room with a coffered ceiling, opposite. The **dress drapes are in teal silk** and the **swags alternate between teal and gold silk. The jabots are done in the gold silk.** The overall effect is both **soft and dramatic!**

Luxurious Shimmer

The **iridescent qualities of the fabrics,** above, play off each other beautifully, creating an **elegant treatment** for a large bay window.

Before

swags

Formal Flair

Heavy damask is a beautiful fabric for a **formal Empire-style look.** The **double swags and shortened jabots** create a valance over dress drapes. The **addition of sheers softens the window** while providing light diffusion for this formal living room.

swags

Command Performance

Grand windows in a grand stairwell call for **grand window treatments!** And there is no better way to dress a formal window than with **beautiful swags and jabots.** The **neutral fabric does not compete with the view,** yet the **elegance of the treatment commands attention.**

Casual Grace Note
From very traditional to quite modern, swag treatments can be used for almost any scheme. This **guest bathroom window** wears a **small printed scarf swag** on top and a **dark-contrast fabric café curtain** on the lower portion. The painted-metal pole has a **leaf finial** in keeping with the green theme. The finished effect is **fun and casual** at the same time.

Before

details

The bottom treatment, above, is a simple one. For privacy, the fabric is opaque, but you can use a sheer if you want more light. The top and bottom of the fabric features a shirred rod-pocket heading. Installation is with two tension rods that are mounted within the window frame.

swags

Past Perfect

Swags are such a **classic and timeless** window treatment that they are used in the hallway of this **historic home** to great effect. Trimming highlights the edges.

Relaxed Look

The combination of a casual fabric and the relaxed drape of these swags provides the perfect balance for this laid-back family room. The swags soften the look of the large, cathedral window without appearing fussy.

Today's Traditional Style

In contrast to the treatment shown on the previous page, **solid-white fabric** and a **structured swag treatment** with **accompanying dress drapes,** above, provide the right look for this room. The scale and fullness of the design, however, brings it up to date.

Pretty Embellishment

This **double-bell jabot,** opposite, is **contrast-lined with a small plaid fabric** that introduces a **casual accent to the formal cream silk. Multicolored tassel fringe** is a lovely way to bring in all the colors that appear in this pretty living room.

Stunning Statement

Shimmer and shine are the essential ingredients of this design, opposite. This **swag is attached to each end ring** so that it can move with the drapes when they are drawn. The **oversize pole and finial** add to the drama. This is a perfect example of how a window treatment can completely rely on the fabric to set the tone of the finished look.

A Neat Fit

This **classic, structured swag-and-jabot treatment,** above, has been installed inside the frame of the window in keeping with **the room's traditional look.**

A Soft Touch

Blue-and-white gathered swags add color and pattern to this all-white kitchen. The **fabric also softens the look** of the functional, but not quite as fanciful, **Venetian blinds.**

snugs

Casual Corner

In another corner of the kitchen shown opposite, this **breakfast nook** has the same window treatment, which unifies the room. This **casual look** is quite **fresh and pretty, and yet easy to maintain.**

Contrasting Interest

Stunning toile fabric dressed with fringe makes a strong impact in this traditional dining room. The **contrast fringe outlines the single swag and cascade jabots** installed over drapes, and the **floor-length sheers** soften the overall effect.

Plush Arrangement

Yards of fabric have been arranged on a pole and tacked in place to create a **double-swag effect** in a unique variation on the theme of a **timeless treatment. Fringe emphasizes the swoop** of the swags and adds glamour.

from inspiration to installation

2) 3'0" WINDOWS 8' CLGS

PLAIN SILK DRAPES W/ BEADS ON ASYMMETRICAL SWAGS

OH POLES FINIALS BY NBI

Glamorous Beading

An asymmetrical swag arranged over drapes features a beaded edge to add glamour to this dining room. The rich fabric looks luxurious.

Before

Problem Solving

Corner windows always pose a problem, and a **clever solution** was to **dress these windows with asymmetrical swag scarves.** A **single tail fills the corner** and **conceals the window trim.** Privacy and light control are provided by a **semiopaque shade.**

details

Corner windows require specific solutions. When there is too little or no room in the corner to dress each window separately, angled corner rods come in handy to create a unified look. For more ideas, see Part Two, "Designs for Difficult Windows."

blinds and shades

They can be part of a layered look or used as a stand-alone treatment.

Sometimes the words "shades" and "blinds" are used interchangeably. Here the word "blinds" is the word used to describe a hard or woven treatment with slats. Among the options available for simple window treatments, fabric shades stand out as the best option. They provide a finished look without being unnecessarily complex. You can choose from flat or soft-fold Roman shades, London shades, balloon shades, or Austrian shades, which are the most popular styles, or others. Each one has a slightly different design that conveys a tailored look through fabric and detail. Combining the best of both worlds, fabric shades are beautiful and classic, and they are easy to operate and maintain.

Venetian (horizontal-slatted) or vertical blinds are some of the most common options for hard window treatments. They can be easily adjusted to control light, air, and privacy. The range of options for color and decorative tape is vast; though these blinds are simple, the variety of choices enables you to personalize a design. You can achieve a look that is casual or formal, simple or complex, or even completely uncluttered for a space that isn't large enough for fabric window treatments. Woven textures are another very popular and beautiful look for blinds—the natural variety in color and texture can bring charm and character to a room.

Low-Key Luxury

One of the client's goals for this dramatic English bedroom, opposite top, was to keep the window treatments simple. A **London shade** made of a beautiful **embroidered silk fabric** meets the needs perfectly. The **edges are bound in a bronze-color fabric for extra contrast and definition.** A quiet corner of the same bedroom, inset, illustrates the shade in a lowered position. Notice how effective **blackout lining** can be.

blinds and shades

Edge Treatment

The **bronze edging** shown below **adds shape to the design.**

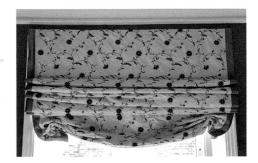

Dressed Up

This kitchen **shade is actually stationary.** Because no privacy or light control is needed, the fabric shade is **decorative rather than functional.** It is a **simple yet effective** way to dress the window.

from inspiration to installation

WHITE
PUCKERED
FABRIC
ROMAN
BLIND

BOUND
W/CARAMEL
COTTON
SATEEN &
TRIMMED W/2
ROWS OF
BRAID

Pretty, Practical Space

The choice of fabric and contrast trim is what makes this soft Roman shade so pretty. The white fabric is "puckered" and the contrast edging is cotton sateen. Both colors are picked up from the floral wallpaper, providing a fresh look in this lady's closet.

details

If you need a more substantial shade or some light filtering, you can order a lined Roman shade. It's a good idea in a walk-in closet or a dressing room.

Mix 'n Match

The **similar tones and colors** in these **complementary patterns,** below, make the **floral valance** work so well with the **plaid Roman shade.**

Strong Lines

A **clean architectural look,** right, is achieved with **tailored shades** that have been installed on the staggered windows' frieze boards, just below the molding. The choice of **plain fabric blends with the white walls,** keeping the space **simple and clean.**

A French Accent

A toile fabric on the windows brings more color and pattern into this room. The fabric is repeated in the chair on the right. When using shades in a window bay, keep the space between each one small—$\frac{1}{4}$ in. maximum.

Clean Canvas

Plain canvas shades make a **statement of simplicity** in this master bedroom. The color of the headboard is picked up as a **contrast band along the bottom edge of the Roman shades.**

details

You can use a contrast band to easily dress up plain shades or drapes. Sometimes the color of the band can be a lighter or darker tone of the main color, or you can choose an entirely different hue picked up from another element in the room.

from inspiration to installation

MINI WHITE ON WHITE EMBROIDERED FLOWERS

W/GLASS BEADS

Bejeweled Design

A balloon shade fabricated with white embroidered fabric adds youthful, feminine appeal to this room. Glass lavender beads, which pick up the wall color, are the ultimate detail for a scalloped edge.

Complex Print

The combination of a lively ivy-print fabric and an elaborate Austrian shade, above, are in direct contrast to the plain Roman shades featured on page 108. Repeating the print in the shower curtain creates a fun and cheerful effect.

Custom Shade

The fabric was laminated to create this stiff, flat-panel roller shade, opposite. This is a great way to use one of the fabrics from a room scheme. A side clutch mechanism makes operation of the shade easy. An upholstered pelmet covers the top of the shade.

A Pampered Look

Soothing colors and the right scale are illustrated in this tasteful bathroom. The plaid cascade shade is simply decorative—mini-blinds control light and privacy.

A Male Perspective

Dark Roman shades give a masculine punch of color to this bedroom. When faced with a challenge such as windows of varying heights, working with the architecture, rather than fighting it, produces the most pleasing result.

blinds and shades

Gathered Together

The side-gathered shades' **large-scale plaid** in tones of **gold, gray, and cream** pulls the color scheme together in this family room.

details

Fabric shades use considerably less fabric than curtains and draperies. So if you're looking for an economical way to add color and pattern to a room, a fabric shade may be the answer. Even a silk shade won't break your budget. Think of it as luxury for less!

details

Pleated and cellular shades do not lend themselves to fancy hems, but some have pretty designs woven into the fabric. Also, some types are insulated for energy efficiency.

Soft and Light

Pleated shades are a **soft alternative to traditional slatted blinds**. These shades have the additional benefit of **diffusing the light**.

blinds and shades

Practical Versatility

Double-cord control, a special option, makes it possible to **move** these shades from the bottom up or from the top down.

Before

Texturous Bamboo
These asymmetrically draped windows are dramatically topped with painted tin pelmets. Layers of metallic paint on recycled tin add depth and texture to the slubbed silk drapes and bamboo blinds.

Earthy Elements

This family room, above, displays the **perfect balance of color and texture.** The strongly colored walls are counterbalanced by **floral drapes. Blackout shades** have been installed under the textured blinds for **complete light control.**

Stylish Shadings

Here is another view of the room with the **under-blinds drawn,** left.

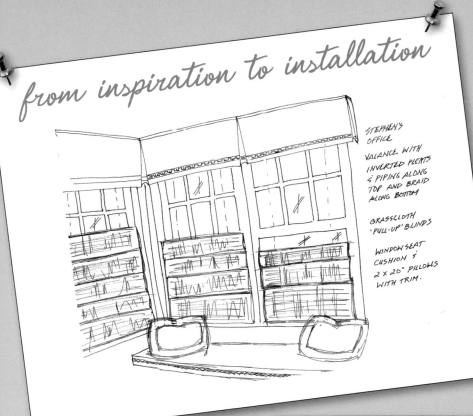

from inspiration to installation

STEPHEN'S OFFICE

VALANCE WITH INVERTED PLEATS & PIPING ALONG TOP AND BRAID ALONG BOTTOM

GRASSCLOTH "PULL-UP" BLINDS

WINDOW SEAT CUSHION 5" 2 X 20" PILLOWS WITH TRIM.

Office Attire

A very tailored look is achieved with low-profile textured grass-cloth blinds that are bottom mounted for privacy control that does not obscure the light. A fresh blue-and-cream-striped valance adds to the crisp feeling of this home office.

Before

Before

Layered Look

This breakfast bay was remodeled with larger windows. The new **translucent treatments** keep the space full of sunshine even though the window is quite "dressed." The **patterned sheers are casually tacked up,** creating a scalloped heading, while the **bamboo shades** hang below the transom window to **allow natural light into the room.** When windows are tall, hanging the blinds below the top prevents the look from appearing overdone.

Balancing Act

This **type of matchstick shade** is **translucent and adds just the right amount of texture and color** to the space. The **patterned drapes contribute weight and warmth** to counterbalance the lightness of the shades. Note the **scalloped edge of the drapes,** a detail that softens the look. Again, striking the right balance between color and texture is important in a window treatment.

details

Natural or woven shades are made of bamboo, sisal, grass cloth, jute, straw, or other exotic grasses and reeds. They are usually neutral, in colors that range from pale straw to dark brown, and sometimes earthy reds and olives. Some, such as bamboo, are made from naturally renewable resources and are therefore earth friendly.

from inspiration to installation

QUILTED FABRIC
PELMET

SUEDE BANDING
1½"

5-6" SPACE

16"

24"

BLACK "PULL-UP"
SOLAR-SHADES

Plain Geometry

For a contemporary look, solar-screen shades look sleek while filtering the sun without obscuring the view. The stepped pelmet is upholstered in a quilted fabric and contrast-bound in suede to enhance the modern feel of this breakfast area.

Natural Beauty

Cheery is the word that comes to mind looking at this fresh sunroom. A **medium-textured blind with a blackout lining** provides a light tone of color at the windows to balance the **strong coral-hued walls and club chair.**

Morning Cheer

Casual teardrop valances and sheer panels, hanging on contrasting poles, dress up the matchstick blinds in this breakfast room, opposite.

A Touching Treatment

The family room, above, shows off lots of color and texture. A bamboo blind adds tactile sophistication to the scheme.

A Warm Note

A **bamboo blind adds a great punch of texture and warmth** to balance
the cool metal and stone surfaces and **almost all-white** scheme in this
kitchen. It also picks up the tones of the wood floor.

Setting the Stage

Natural hardwood blinds control the light and privacy in a room designed for an active family. Because floor-length drapes would have been impractical, a **curved valance with pinch pleats** was chosen to add a **dash of color** and to frame the window.

details

Wood blinds always add warmth to a room. Furthermore, they can be painted or stained to match or contrast with other furnishings or trimwork. To add a custom touch, consider a fashionable color or patterned fabric tape that coordinates with the rest of the window treatment.

blinds and shades

An Easy Choice

Light filters through the
white blinds, opposite,
casting a lively pattern on
the **"under-the-sea" mural**
in this **child's bathroom.**

Unique Detail

The convenience of a **Venetian
blind** in a bathroom is hard to
beat because it is easy to operate
and maintain. For personal style,
a **clever border of real birch
branches** frames the window
opening, above.

On the Border

This **creative treatment of an
unframed window,** left, was
simply tacked around the opening.

Added Potential

White blinds complement the **white-painted built-in bookcases,** opposite, and provide the most basic type of coverage, leaving room for a soft curtain or valance.

Updated Elegance

Off-white **tailored woven shades** are a practical choice in this bedroom, below. **Silk drapes flanking the window bay** add elegance. They can be drawn when more privacy is desired.

Minis to the Max

Miniblinds almost blend into the background when paired with a soft sheer over-drape. Ease of operation and light control make these types of blinds very popular.

Soft Note

A **blue and white valance** adds a cheery note and dresses up the look of **plain white blinds** on French doors in a young girl's room. A valance is a good way to soften the look of a hard treatment.

blinds and shades

Blind Ambition

The **wood tone of the blinds above supplies the warmth needed** in a large basement family room. Because blinds are easily adjustable, they're a **smart choice in a room designed for TV** and movie viewing.

Tailored Touch

In a **home office,** these **wood blinds, right, coordinate with the room's bookcases.** Textured chenille fabric covers the **shaped, upholstered pelmet, edged with a contrasting black cord** for a crisp, clean look.

details

Venetian blinds are versatile, but they can be difficult to clean unless you dust the slats every few days. If grime accumulates, you will have to take them down for cleaning in a bathtub filled with warm soapy water. You can rinse them in the shower. Let them air dry on a clean towel.

Attractive Pair

Blinds are an excellent choice when privacy is a concern. **White Venetian blinds hang under casual swags, which soften the look.** The extra height of these windows adds to the **elegant effect.**

blinds and shades

Functional Matters

The sleekness of this contemporary
kitchen calls for a **clean-lined
window treatment. Painted-white wood
blinds** are easy to operate and clean,
which is especially important in a kitchen.

A Warm Tone

A dark wood-tone blind adds a strong accent color that picks up the hue of the trunk in front of the sofa. For a finishing touch, the stationary brown-and-white-check fabric shade (and matching throw pillows) completes the look.

from plain to personality plus

pelmets and valances

Use them to soften a hard treatment, hide hardware, or correct proportions.

Pelmets and valances are short treatments installed at the top of the window used to hide drapery hardware. A pelmet—an upholstered cornice—can be a great addition to an existing hard or soft window treatment, or it can make a simple statement on its own. Made of an upholstered, shaped board, a pelmet is a top treatment that presents an opportunity to interject fabric, style, and color to a simple design in any room in the house.

Fabric valances come in as many styles as there are headings or pleats. Essentially a mini curtain made to dress the top portion of a window, a valance can be used alone or as a top treatment over long drapes, shades, blinds, or shutters. Valances are the easiest way to introduce fabric to a window without going over the top. Select an overall shape or profile to suit the window and style in the room; then pick a pleat or heading, go to town with optional trimmings, or leave the valance plain.

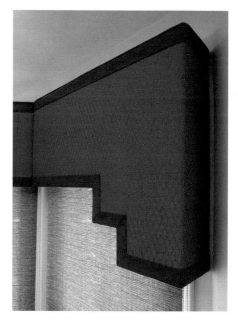

Right Angles

A close-up detail of this **stepped valance** illustrates the importance of good craftsmanship in the workroom. The **contrast band** of fabric **provides crisp delineation of the shape.**

from inspiration to installation

SHAPED, UPHOLSTERED PELMET WITH BEADS

FABRIC ROMAN BLIND

Distinctive Design

This window is the focal point in this onyx master bath. A Roman blind was installed under a uniquely shaped pelmet to add a punch of color. The unique shape of the pelmet was carefully designed to show off the pattern in the fabric.

details
A pelmet or a valance can be used to elongate or widen a window's proportions.

pelmets and valances

Shapely Silhouette

Striped fabric, opposite, enhances these **valances with curved tops and arched bottoms.** Simple shirring provides enough fullness for the valance, which has been trimmed with a **knotted cord along the gathers** and **scalloped at the bottom edge.** The combination provides a pleasing frame for the tall windows.

Bottoms Up

This **shaped valance,** below, frames the top portion of the window. **Matching fabric** was used to create the **bottom-mounted pleated shade.** Using a **blind that operates from the bottom up** is a clever solution next to a bathtub where privacy is needed on the lower half of the window.

Floral Formality

Working with the pattern of this **floral fabric,** I created a **scalloped shape for the upholstered pelmet.** A dash of color was added with the **blue contrast banding.** A dark-cream-color **blackout roller shade** addresses practical needs.

Before

Thread Flair

A close-up of this pretty, **embroidered-silk pelmet,** left, shows **wider-than-usual piping.** You can see the folds of the drape below the valance and catch a peek of the **Roman blind.**

Contour Culture

The **undulating shape of the valance,** below, adds interest to the design.

from inspiration to installation

35" WIDE

35" HIGH

4" RETURN

SHAPED UPHOLSTERED PELMET
FLORAL CREWEL W/PIPING
ON INSIDE EDGES

High Minded

The light color of this pelmet contrasts sharply with the dark color of the walls. The floral pattern is an explosion of vines, and this pelmet is just big enough to show off the full pattern. The fun shape adds a lot of interest to this dead-end hall space.

details

You can create a pelmet in your desired shape. Elaborate curves, for example, add richness to the treatment, especially when the fabric is luxurious.

pelmets and valances

Return Style

I was able to repurpose some of a client's drapery, which was being replaced, to create this design. The **pelmet** was done in a **geometric shape to echo the lines of the dormer window.**

details

Because a pelmet is created from stiffened fabric, you can create any one of various shapes for the bottom edge, including sawtooth (pictured), pennant, notched, scalloped, or teardrop.

On Point

A **sawtooth edge,** above, was designed to work with the **diamond pattern** in this **tailored fabric.** The depth of color and pattern does not require any additional embellishment.

Softly Structured

This **tea-stained floral,** opposite, has **two pleats that are held up with decorative braid** at the ends. This creates a curve along the bottom edge, giving the valance the **effect of a London blind.**

Fetching Floral
The photo at left shows
the **valance's floral pattern**
and **pleat detail.**

pelmets and valances

All Ruffles

A bell-and-swag valance is trimmed in blue with a scalloped top and a contrast fabric and button for the tab heading. It hangs over a decorative pole. Contrast trim defines the bottom edges and echoes the trim used on the bedskirt. Typically, a pattern or a strong color is recommended for a room with white walls, but all the ingredients come together beautifully.

Matching Motif
**A scalloped bottom adds a feminine touch
to this valance.** The **yellow floral print** is
used on both the quilted bedspread and the
windows for a unified look.

pelmets and valances

revealing idea

This blue-and-white toile valance has a smocked heading and is trimmed with matching tassel fringe. It is secured to a dust board with hook-and-loop fastening tape. A dust board, which is also called a "valance board," is a cornice-like structure without front or side panels.

Draped Look

This **bell-and-swag valance** is **installed on a dust board** to allow the fabric to fall straight down from the top **for a draped tablecloth look.**

Top Chic

A small valance in a strong color creates a frame at the window without blocking the view or the light. The lower half of the windows has a lightweight sheer, which directs all of the interest on the valance.

Casual Elegance

Subtle earth-tone toile fabric complements this breakfast nook, where a **swagged valance** is pulled up at the pleats and looped over a **barley-twist wrought-iron pole.**

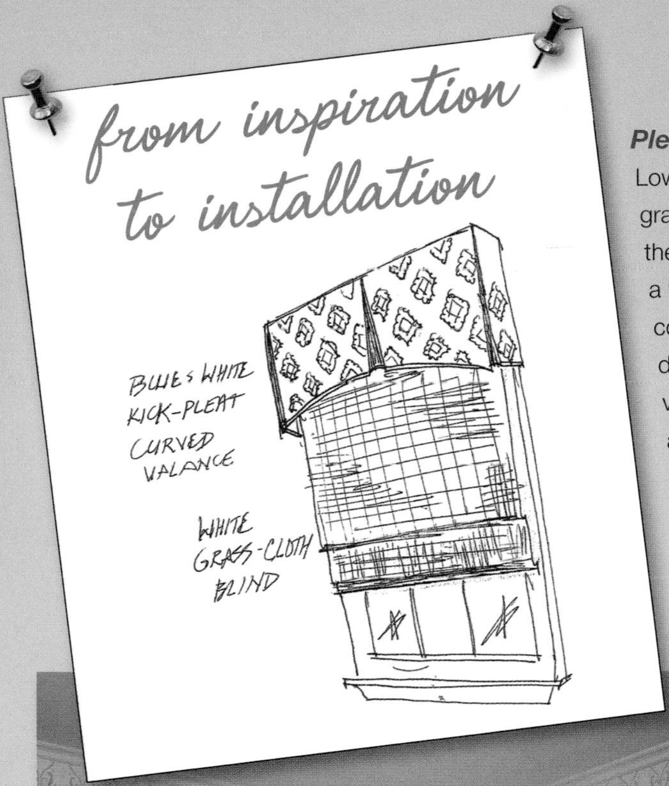

from inspiration to installation

BLUE & WHITE
KICK-PLEAT
CURVED
VALANCE

WHITE
GRASS-CLOTH
BLIND

Pleated Details

Low-textured, slat-like white grass-cloth blinds, paired with the patterned wallpaper, add a feminine look to this quiet corner. Note the kick-pleat detail in the curved valance—it adds interest to a plain window without appearing fussy.

Complete Picture

A box-pleated valance with a tone-on-tone trim accompanies these formal drapes. Using a rich butterscotch-color fabric complements the wallpaper, creating a pretty look at the window.

from plain to personality plus

shutters and screens

Alone or paired with a soft treatment, shutters and screens offer more options for dressing windows with style.

More than any other window treatment, shutters bring an architectural element into a room. Other window treatments may look merely like a fashion choice; shutters, once installed, appear to be part of the home's basic character, much like crown molding and floorboards.

Shutters can be installed inside the window frame or outside the window opening within a frame of their own. Depending on the size of the window, they can be installed as a single shutter that swings open to one side of the window; as a pair that opens in the center, or as four or more panels that are hinged together and split at the center.

Shutters offer various options for privacy; they can cover all or just the lower portion of the window. They are also a good buffer against noise, which makes them perfect for street-level rooms.

Louvers, the vertical and horizontal slats that give shutters their character, come in standard widths: $1\frac{1}{4}$, $1\frac{3}{4}$, $2\frac{1}{2}$, $3\frac{1}{2}$, and $4\frac{1}{2}$ inches. Wide louvers allow more sunlight into a room when they are open, while narrow slats provide some screening in this position.

There are also fabric-insert shutters that allow you to add more color or pattern than the traditional painted or stained wood types. A sun-resistant, light- to medium-weight fabric is a good choice.

Shoji screens consist of a translucent panel set into a wood frame. This type of treatment is well suited to a modern or Asian-inspired design. Screens usually slide open on a track, but they can also be hinged to work like a shutter.

Light and Informal
Plantation shutters can be evocative of beach cottages and are a **perfect solution for this casual setting.**

Café Shutters

Using **shutters on the lower half of a window** is an option when full-height privacy is not an issue. This way, **light can always flood the room** during the day.

*from inspiration
to installation*

KNOTTED
WHITE
CORD

RED CANVAS
VALANCE
TRIMMED W/WHITE
CORD

FULL HT. WHITE
SHUTTERS

MOUNT VALANCE @ CLG SO
SHUTTERS CAN OPEN & CLOSE

Top Treatment

For a client that wanted a consistent look from the outside, shutters were installed in all of the bedrooms and bathrooms along the front of the house. In the young boy's bedroom, I added a punch of color with a red valance that is trimmed with white cord. It is a great look, and because the valance was actually installed above the top of the window, the shutters are easy to operate.

details

Shutters are usually constructed of pine. They can be painted or stained any color; some styles are available prepainted in standard and custom colors.

A Custom Fit

These **clean, white louvers,** left, are a fresh addition to this **young girl's bathroom.** Because the window is small, a **single shutter** was all that was needed.

Plain Practical

Keep it simple. In the bathroom, opposite, a **pair of shutters** with 1¾-in. slats **does not compete with the faux painting for attention.**

Stacked Treatment

The black-and-white toile bathroom, right, called for the **crisp contrast of white shutters.** Separate units on the top and bottom of the window **offer more options for light, air, and privacy.**

Masculine Chic

A strong masculine statement is made with these dark shutters in "his" master bath. The brown wood tone picks up the color of the accent tiles. As always, shutters provide easy light and privacy control, which is particularly important here because the windows flank the vanity mirror.

Natural Calm

The **quintessential shoji screen adds a Zen-like ambiance** to this low key master bedroom, opposite. Leaving the top of this large window bare keeps the space open to **natural light and a view of the trees.**

Asian-Modern Fusion

Sliding shoji screens, below, provide a contemporary option to the ubiquitous suburban sliding door. The style makes a wonderful statement in this smart-looking **bedroom with Asian accents.**

Screen Solution

Good-looking screens can make a statement both inside and outside the home. In this case, they add an important design element to this living room and conceal windows that do not match the decor.

window treatments and color

Moods are affected, feelings are evoked, and complete environments are determined by color.

Color is a key element in design, whether you are choosing it for the walls or the windows. Without it, a room cannot be complete. Color is also a way for you to inject your personal style into a room, a way to express yourself and make a space truly yours. Color can indicate the purpose or the mood of a room. The emotions and memories evoked by a certain color can personalize the space further. Bright colors bring cheer each time you walk into a room, while warmer, darker colors create a cozy, comfortable feeling. Sunny yellow or sea green, for example, speak to summer days, cheery breakfasts, and time outdoors while maroon, deep green, and navy create an feeling of security. When you're choosing a color, whether it is for the walls or the window treatments, think of how you want to feel when you are in that room. Neutrals can open up a small room visually, but more often than not, it is bold color that enhances the natural beauty of a space, whatever its size.

Color is nothing to fear, especially if you want to bring it into a room with the window treatment. For a bold approach, solid-color drapes can make the windows a focal point while contrasting trim or accents can play off the dominant scheme, pulling together the entire design for a cohesive look.

When you're selecting a color, just think about the overall mood you want to establish and give some consideration to the colors that always make your heart sing. Don't over analyze a color, just react to it. Trust your gut feeling.

Good as Gold
The **color of these walls and drapes** was **inspired by gold flecks in the beautiful marble countertop.** The leading edge of the drapes is **accented with a plaid fabric band.**

from inspiration to installation

LG. WINDOW IN FAMILY ROOM

SCALLOPED
VALANCE
WITH 3
SOFT FOLDS
& BRAID @
SEAMS

TEXTURED
GRASS-CLOTH
BLINDS BY
OTHERS

DRESS DRAPES
WITH PINCH
PLEATS

Before

Harvest Hues

A larger view of this family room reveals the rich tones of the floral drape fabric, which was the starting point for all of the colors and textures—a sofa upholstered in brown chenille, a burgundy animal-print loveseat, and an ottoman covered in faux ostrich leather for durability.

FAMILY ROOM
FRENCH DOORS

CROWN MOLDING

GOBLET PLEATED
DRAW DRAPES

from inspiration to installation

2 SMALL WINDOWS IN FAMILY ROOM

2 VALANCES W/TEXTURED GRASS-CLOTH BLINDS BELOW

BUILT-IN BOOKCASES

CUSTOM FIREPLACE W/COLUMNS

BUILT-IN BOOKCASES

Before

Naturally Warm

There is a bounty of earth tones in this remodeled family room. The tea-stained fabric valances with grass-cloth blinds complement the deep tan walls and leather chair, making this room a study in natural textures and earthy colors.

Draped Dramatically

Strongly colored **raspberry walls** are **accented with deep burgundy drapes.** This window treatment has three layers for added impact: **dress drapes, sheers** that are **used as an under-drape, and a textured grass-cloth blind.**

Upbeat Palette

This cheery family room relies on the **timeless color combination of blue (as seen in the drapes) and yellow for impact.** Additional accents were added with a **green armoire** and a **large-patterned chair fabric.**

window treatments and color

Fun Stuff

This **baseball-themed bedroom** is a lovely
pairing of color and texture. The **playful valance
has a tab hem that holds a baseball bat.** The
dark-green wall is a good color choice for a
display of sports paraphernalia.

Wow Factor

This sophisticated dining room with tone-on-tone striped navy walls features a textured-woven fabric in gold for the window treatments. The gold offers a strong contrast to the walls and picks up tones in the rug.

Naturally Neutral

Color can also be expressed in **neutral hues,** such as **shades of white and cream**. This restrained palette, right, creates a serene escape.

Strong Statement

Pattern, color, and more pattern abound in this **cozy lodge-like bedroom,** below. The red walls are repeated in the red plaid bedding while the **green check provides a great contrast!** It's a wonderful study in color and pattern.

Delicate Design

It's so pretty in pink! A **pink scalloped pelmet** frames the window, opposite. Underneath, there is a **yellow blind** that echoes the wall color. Notice that the **blind is trimmed in pink,** which was taken from the color of the pelmet. The complete "package" makes a sweet treatment for a **young girl's bedroom.**

Red Curtain

Red provides the perfect punch of color for this **asymmetrically dressed window,** above, in a girl's bathroom.

Before

Rich Reward

Deep salmon-color striped drapes, above, add a lively punch of color in a café-au-lait home office. Note how the pleats work consistently with the repeat of the stripes, forming a **consistent panel of color on the outside fold of each pleat.**

Low-Key Look

Earth tones found in the wallpaper, right, are picked up in the woven texture of the **café curtain and gathered valance.** The **open weave of the fabric** also adds interest.

Floral Frills

A **floral valance in blue and yellow** adds just the right youthful touch here. Light and privacy are controlled with the **crisp-white matchstick blinds.**

details

Warm colors appear to advance, making a room feel more intimate. Conversely, cool colors and neutrals seem to recede, which will visually open up small spaces.

Go for It

The contrast of the **blue drapes against the yellow walls** is a bold
choice. Rings allow the drapes to move back and forth easily on the rod,
enabling easy adjustment of the **white plantation shutters.**

Worth Repeating
Repetition of color is a very effective tool for impact. In this lovely child's bedroom, the yellow and blue plaid repeats the color scheme, which is also picked up in the window seat, chair, and throw pillows.

Modern Scheme

Neutral-color textured drapes add a note of elegance to this contemporary living room. The **grommet heading is a clean-lined solution** for a modern look. In this situation, using color at the windows would have thrown off the desired effect, but a dash of it here and there in the throw pillows and on the accent chairs is just right.

window treatments and color

Before

patterns and prints

A pattern or print on the window treatment can add excitement to a solid-color room.

For the color-shy client, patterns and prints are a safe way to experiment. They also provide a great opportunity to express your preferences and personality. I often find that I can learn a lot about my clients from their reaction to certain patterns, prints, and colors. Some people love plaids; others hate them. The same can be said of striped, toile, or floral motifs. Fabric prints really have to suit the individual. Deciding what patterns you like is an important precursor to choosing fabrics for your home. Birds often cause a visceral reaction in people—some people will simply "not have them in their home!" Others like their flowers "only in vases," while some clients tell me that they simply "love anything with circles!" For the record, I love plaids, can happily live with birds, and I don't mind flowers on my fabrics. ◆

Think about homes you admire, magazines you like, even the clothing you wear before you commit to a print or a color for your home. However you decide to approach the window treatments, whether your taste is classic or modern, bold, experimental, or basic, there is something that is perfect for you.

A Classic French-Country Print
The freshness of a **blue-and-white toile print** is timeless. In this master bedroom, extra depth of color is added with **dark-blue wallpaper.** Cream provides balance for the color and pattern to create a **soothing place of repose.**

Before

Mixing Prints

Multiple patterns and strong colors make up the palette for this lively formal living room, right. The drapery fabric echoes the medallion pattern of the rug. Two stripes of varying proportions dress the chairs and tablecloth.

Balancing the Scale

Scale is one of the main considerations when you're mixing multiple patterns. It's best to combine different-size prints, usually reserving the larger motif for the larger surface or, in the case below, a curtain. The small scale of the print on the café curtain is the perfect partner to the large scale on the dress drape.

Pleasant Palette

Softer tones of a **pale yellow and a light blue** create a very fresh and lovely setting for this sunny sitting room, left. All the tonal values of the colors work well together. The **tack-pleated floral drapes add the pattern,** while the **solid-color sofa provides an anchor** in the room.

Lively Pattern

Blue-and-tan plaid adds a cheerful note to this breakfast area, below. The **plaid is used on the diagonal** in the **fall-over heading** and the **single valance,** creating contrast and interest.

patterns and prints

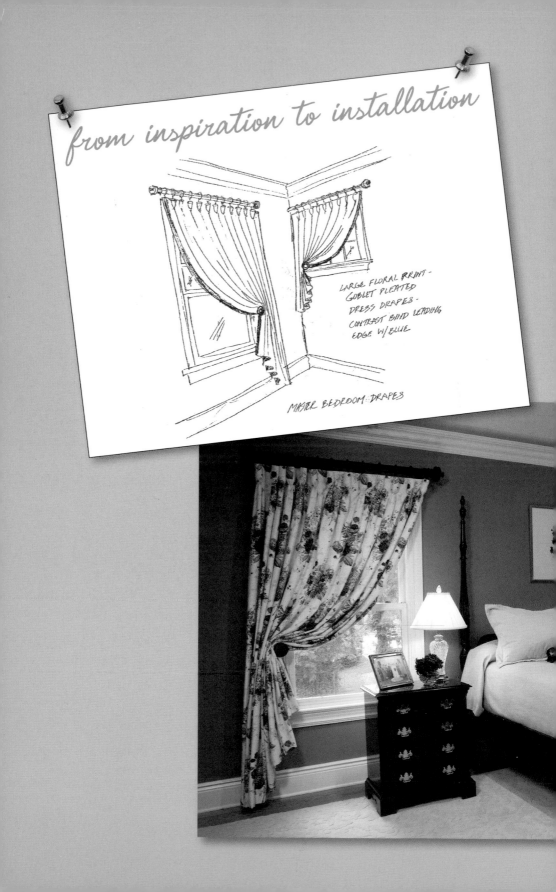

from inspiration to installation

LARGE FLORAL PRINT -
GOBLET PLEATED
DRESS DRAPES -
CONTRAST BAND LEADING
EDGE W/BLUE

MASTER BEDROOM DRAPES

Garden Inspired

Red, white, and blue floral drapes add a traditional touch to this master bedroom and enliven the entire space. The tone of blue in the drapes is picked up in a contrast-bound edge and complements the walls beautifully. Note the pattern in the fabric.

Before

from plain to personality plus

Front and Center

To show off a pretty fabric print, these valances hang flat across the top of the windows, below. The scalloped curtain-ring heading and scalloped bottom edge enhance the look, and plain white sheers allow the yellow, black, and white top treatment to take all the attention.

Call of the Wild

Animal prints are a timeless and fun way to invigorate any room. A matching blind and shower curtain, opposite, make a large style statement in this small bathroom.

So Much Fun

Children's rooms call for **bright patterns,** and this **lively, colorful cityscape print** creates such a happy look. The fabric's adorable print shows off well as a **flat-fold Roman shade,** even in a raised position.

patterns and prints

details

Patterns may repeat vertically or horizontally. You have to know the exact length and width of each repeat to match the pattern precisely.

Perfect Match

This is an example of how important it is to **carefully match the pattern** when you are **combining a pelmet and a fabric shade**. The **attention to detail** pays off when you see how **crisp and seamless** the finished window treatment looks.

Country Retreat

The yellow-and-blue floral pattern chosen for the drapes and shade creates a cheerful mood in this guest suite. With the plaid draped tablecloth and the striped cushion and pillow on the window seat, the mix draws together a cozy, cottage look.

patterns and prints

Show It Off

When you are working with a large patterned fabric, play with it. Running the pattern horizontally on the pelmet and vertically on the blinds, left, permits you to see and appreciate the overall design. Notice how the pattern gets buried in the gathers of dress drapes.

Attention Grabbing

The toile print chosen for this window treatment, below, is accented with a fringe on the shaped upholstered pelmet. The same print was duplicated for the headboard. A contrasting but complementary pattern was selected for the bedskirts.

sheers

These versatile curtains offer a lightweight alternative to heavy drapes, or they can be part of a layered treatment.

Sheers are made of translucent fabric, such as voile, cotton lace, or a loosely woven polyester. The perfect choice for a casual window treatment when you want something that is airy and summery, sheers don't block the light completely. They offer some screening, allowing you to see what's happening outside your window while blocking the view into your home from the outside. These curtains can be plain or fancy, featuring stripes, appliqués, and lacy patterns. They come in many colors. Use them alone or in combination with another window treatment, such as a pretty valance. Pair a patterned sheer or lace with a plain weave, or combine them with drapes for a layered look. You can also use sheers to soften the look of hard blinds. Some sheer fabrics can be used to create a lightweight fabric shade.

So just when you thought that sheers were boring, you will discover that they are quite versatile and attractive.

Light Touch
A striped sheer is used for an Austrian shade over the tub, left, which is part of a luxurious spa.

Airy Retreat
The same striped sheer used at left is a subtle way to add interest to these French doors, opposite, while keeping the narrow space light. A simple sheer London shade, trimmed with a ribbon-loop fringe, provides a classic look.

Sheer Beauty
Embroidered sheers
are a lovely way to
**introduce color
and pattern** while
maintaining a **light
overall feeling.** Such
rich sheers are **strong
enough to handle
fringe** and elaborate
treatments, whereas
more lightweight
fabrics can be too
delicate.

sheers

Gather Together

The **hourglass sheer,** above, is a fun way to treat windows. Here, a **contrast fabric is used for the band that secures the gathers** of this whimsical treatment.

Simple Style

White hourglass sheers, opposite, repeated in a series of windows over the tub, **add interest to these casement windows.** The classic windows called for an **elegant yet simple treatment.**

sheers

sheers

Handsome Pair

The use of **two-tone sheers,** left, creates the illusion of a formal treatment—**dark-tone dress drapes and light-tone draw drapes.** Yet, the **overall feeling is still quite casual** in this room thanks to the fabric. The darker sheer fabric is also used for the shade on the single window.

Sheer Delight

Ultimate drama is created by **lining the walls and ceiling** of this dressing room, below, with **shirred sheer fabric.** The lightness of the fabric is a perfect choice for this **feminine space.**

Light and Bright

Crisp white sheers are secured to a swing-arm rod with rope in this **nautical-themed room.**

from inspiration to installation

TEXTURED METAL PELMET — BY OTHERS

2 DROPS OF "METALLIC" SHEER

TEXTURED BEADS

HOLD-BACK BY HBI.

Problem Solver

The offset radiator posed a problem when choosing a window treatment here, so an asymmetrical drape was the only way to go. An iridescent double-layer sheer fabric filters the light beautifully into this front hall. The leading edge is trimmed with raffia-wrapped bobble fringe for further interest.

Before

Before

Lightened Up

The **hint of brown stripes in the sheer fabric** picks up the **warm colors in the room,** above, and adds just enough oomph to the windows. The **overall look is very light** for a naturally dark room.

Lively Sheers

Brown striped sheers are a **fun way to add color and pattern** at the window without a heavy treatment. The heading is just shirred over a chunky pole for a **casual look. Decorative metal holdbacks** create a nice curve to the drapes in the center.

By the Light of the Window

A **sheer white London blind allows light to flow freely** into this attic space below. **Soft blue tones** on the window seat and pillows **create a place for quiet reflection.**

Pattern of Light

Patterned sheers are used for the **soft-fold Roman shade** in this formal living room, above. The colors work beautifully with the dress drapes and the wall color to **create a soft glow of light at the windows.**

sheers

Before

details

You can give added interest to sheer panels with ribbon or braid edgings and interesting headings, or use tiebacks with them to create a graceful shape.

sheers

Soft Scoop

Sheers can be associated with casual window
treatments, but these **formal sill-length swags
and jabots,** opposite, illustrate the versatility of
this wonderful fabric. The width of the jabots
creates a **more finished look.**

Morning Light

Sheer roller blinds make a **contemporary statement** in this breakfast area, above.
When a space calls for a **clutter-free treatment,** roller blinds are a great solution.
The use of a **sheer fabric is quite refreshing** as it filters the light so well.

details

Any sheer window treatment can incorporate blackout shades that will provide total privacy and darkness when you need it.

Billowy Effect

A **contrast satin band gives body and definition** to the edge of this **informally arranged swag treatment,** opposite. **Black decorative holdbacks** are used to wrap and drape the curtain, creating **a touch of drama** along the top.

Special Effect

A **sunburst sheer with a center fabric rosette** is the perfect solution for this pretty powder room, below. These windows are challenging at the best of times and the choice of a **sheer fabric to filter the light** is a good one.

Baby Soft

A **cloud shade in a patterned sheer fabric** creates fullness at this window, left, while still **keeping the look simple.** Light control is provided by a **blackout blind behind the sheer shade.** A bed canopy in a plain sheer is draped over the crib to create a dramatic setting.

Dramatic Drape

A **classic, tack-pleated sheer** is the backdrop for this **dramatic asymmetrical drape with a swag and tassel fringe,** above. The sheer under-curtain is hung on a standard traverse rod while the decorative dress drape hangs from a pole.

trimmings

These finishing touches add flair to a window treatment.

Trimmings can play an important role in creating a look for your window treatments. The decorative embellishments that you choose to accent your window decor can give your design a rich custom look. Delicate, beaded trimmings can beautifully edge silken window drapes, while whimsical large wooden beads can trim a heavy fabric, and a colorful pom-pom trim can add a playful accent in a child's room. Trim can either accentuate the colors and style of the existing design or introduce a new hue to the palette. It's a decision that can reflect the personality of the client—that's you! A stylistically adventurous person who loves color might choose a dramatic red leather fringe to offset curtains in a dining room, while someone who is traditionally inclined may choose a subtle accent that almost blends into the existing fabric. In either case, using trim, tassels, fringe, or beads can put a finishing touch on your window treatments. Besides, trimmings are such fun to select. Also, these embellishments are guaranteed to make your window treatments look professionally designed.

Glamour at the Top

Bronze brush fringe, above, highlights the **formal swag and jabots,** accenting the colors of the **silk plaid.**

Formal and Refined

An **elegant ribbon tieback** and **delicate pearl braid,** opposite, add the perfect touch for this **silk drape.**

Added Oomph
This **sumptuous tieback** has a **chenille pouf above the strands of the main tieback.** It's pure indulgence!

trimmings

Luxury to the Limit

Red tassel fringe outlines these **swag and jabots,**
providing a **crisp edge to this fabric.**

Extra Touch

Navy-and-white tiebacks provide a **polished look**
for these **toile drapes with laminated roller blinds.**

trimmings

Bejeweled

These **lavender glass beads,** above, are just so pretty. The **trim itself is scalloped,** and it forms the edge at the bottom of an **Austrian blind, which is also scalloped.**

Finishing Detail

A **matching red tieback,** right, completes the look.

Fringe Benefit
This **ribbon-loop fringe** has been applied to the folded-back return of this **lambrequin,** left, providing a **contrasting, frivolous note.**

Pretty Fluff
Tasseled multitone fringe dangles playfully from this shapely valance, right. The colors pick up shades in the **floral fabric.**

Fine Tailoring

Cord that **matches the striped fabric** edges the top of this swag. Note how the **cord is knotted at the corner detail,** which is gathered and tacked above the line of the main treatment.

details

Acessories, such as piping, banding, or braid, can be used to neaten unfinished edges or to add a graphic line to a plain treatment, especially when the trim is in a contrasting color, print, or texture.

trimmings

Maltese Cross

A banana-shaped tieback is accented by a decorative rosette, opposite. **A rosette** is a clever way to dress up a curtain tieback.

Border Detail

Using a **braid** horizontally, right, is a **smart way to break up the stripes** of a fallover heading.

From Plain to Pretty

Contrast fabric piping outlines the striped door pelmet and **bead-and-tassel fringe outlines the roller blind,** below. This is a great way to add zip to a functional treatment. Fringe can **turn a plain look into something gorgeous.**

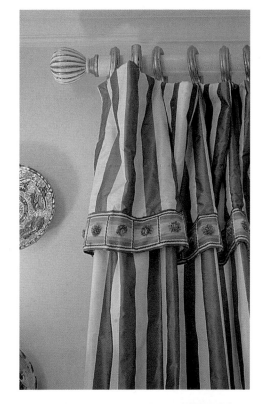

trim, fringe, and tassels

Passementerie, or tassels and trimmings, encompass a range of interlaced, braided, and fringed decorations that have been used traditionally to enhance window treatments. Quality and price vary, depending on whether a trim is made by hand or machine. The type of thread used—silk, linen, viscose, or cotton—also influences cost. Here is a tiny sampling of the vast array of styles and colors.

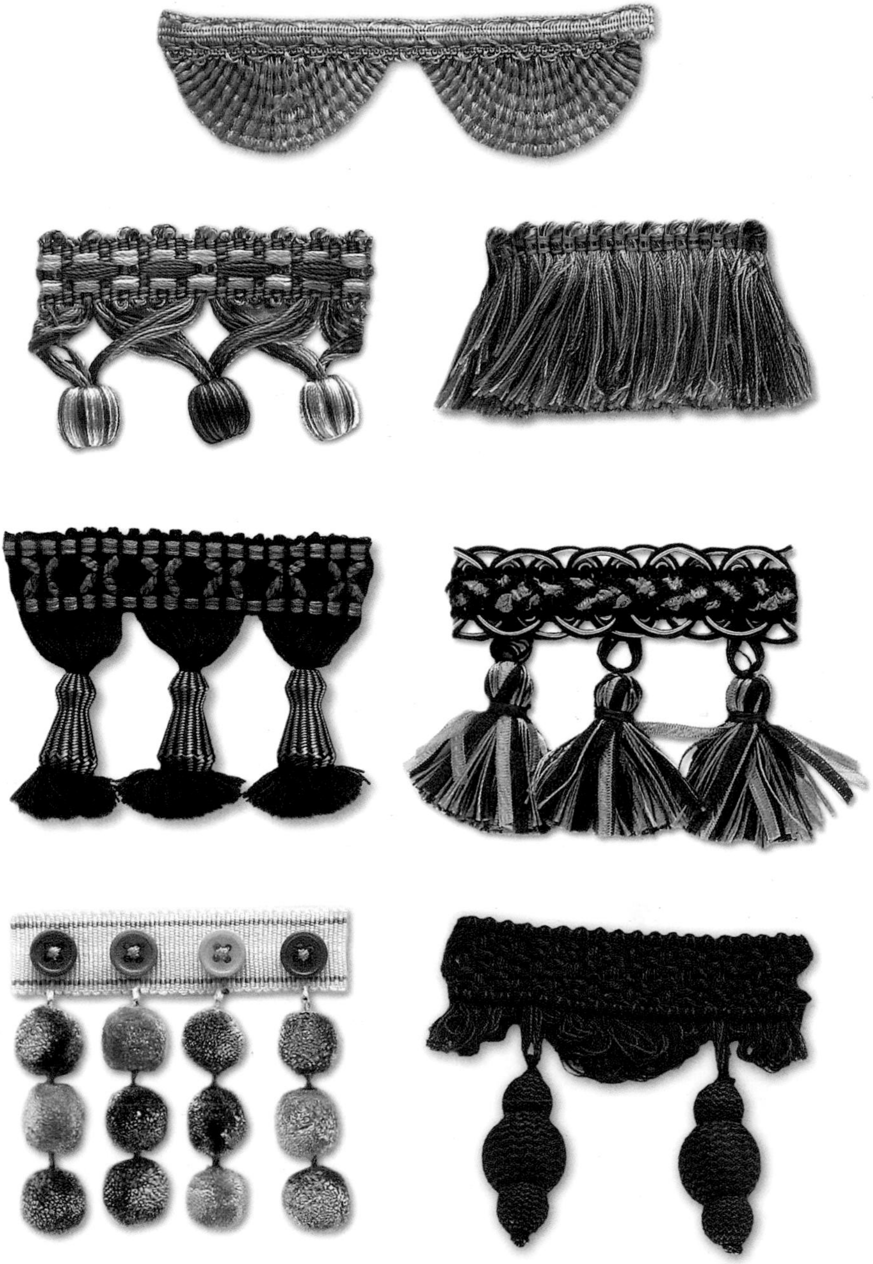

All the Trimmings
The **attached heading,** left, is **curved down from the center with goblet pleats** and then dressed with **tassel fringe** that pick up the colors in the room's rug.

Opulent Look
Bullion fringe, opposite, is a **dramatic way to trim swags and jabots.** The color is perfect for this **classic floral fabric.**

Knotted Tassel Cord

A **two-tone red bullion tieback** echoes the colors featured in this **crewel fabric.**

from inspiration to installation

WINDOW 48" W + 12" STACK EACH SIDE

72"

CLG. HT- APPROX 9'

DROP ≈ 8'4"

VERY FULL SILK DRAPES WITH CRYSTAL BEADS

DRESS IN ELEGANCE
PLAIN CREAM SILK FABRIC 54" W/ CRYSTAL BEADS.

NOT SURE IF WE CAN MAKE THINGS POOL ON FLOOR?

details

Beads can be used to add color, sparkle, and a three-dimensional element to your window treatment's design. You can use glass beads, crystals, or pearls.

Shimmering Crystals

These luxurious silk drapes are drawn back to reveal pretty crystal beading along the edge of each panel.

Before

from inspiration to installation

LIVING ROOM DRAPES

SILK STRIPE
DRESS DRAPES
WITH RED BEADED
TRIM DOWN
LEADING EDGE
ON POLES & FINIALS

Dazzling Enhancement
Beautiful silk striped dress drapes have been enhanced with beads that run down the leading edge of each panel.

Before

trimmings

Rich Tieback

This **brown "horse's mane" tieback,** left, adds a **touch of whimsy** to the **handsome velvet and linen drape.**

Lovely Finishing Detail

Brush fringe down the leading edge is a smart detail for the draw drapes, below. The three **colors work beautifully** with the **floral drapes.** Note the taupe contrast button at the base of the goblet pleats.

details

Fringe can be made of twisted cut, uncut, or looped cords. You can also have fringe custom-dyed to match a specific color in your curtain's fabric.

from plain to personality plus

designer hardware

There is an endless array of poles, finials, and holdbacks that can add to the custom look of a design.

As in each step of the design process, a vast number of choices exist in hardware. Depending on the style of window treatment, hardware can fade into the background or play a central role in the overall design. In fact, it can even act as an accessory that reinforces the design theme of a room. Decorative accent pieces and finials can add interest to otherwise simple curtains. Holdbacks, whether functional or simply decorative, can achieve a similar effect. In each case, many options exist.

Hardware is also a great way to experiment. If bold color or pattern is not to your liking, a metal or intricately carved wooden finial could be a way to add your personal touch.

Different wood finishes are yet another choice you have to make in designing your own window treatments. You can choose between various metals—bronze, pewter, wrought iron, chrome, and nickel, to name the most common types—or solid wood designs in everything from mahogany to maple, or painted finishes. Again, the choice is yours as to whether you want the hardware to blend into the rest of the room or serve as a contrasting accent.

details

Are your windows too short? Visually lengthen them by positioning the drapery hardware above the window trim or close to the ceiling.

On Track

This **fruitwood barley-twist pole** has a **traverse mechanism,** which is a track system that precludes the need for rings. This is the **easiest type of drapery hardware to operate.**

designer hardware

details

Heavy window treatments, such as draperies, require a rod that can support their weight. However, you can safely pair lightweight treatments, such as café curtains or sheers, with a thin rod.

Full-Dress Regalia

Antiqued poles and finials, below, provide the **right degree of formality** for this living room.

Finishing Note

A close-up of the finial, opposite, reveals how **the drape "returns" to the wall.** When curtains simply hang straight, without a return, the look is sloppy because you can see behind the drapery panel.

designer hardware

All That Glitters

This **oversize, 3-in. pole-and-ball finial,** opposite top, features a **gold-leaf finish.** This **touch of glamour** emphasizes the jewel tones in the drapery fabric.

Lustrous Design

An **antiqued-gold pole and finial** pick up the color of the swag's fabric, opposite bottom, providing a **polished look** for this formal dining room.

Updated Look

A **thin wrought-iron pole and finial,** above, add a **contemporary look** to the window treatment that **does not compete with the drapes.**

details

Decorative holdbacks fabricated in metal, wood, or glass present another opportunity for embellishment. Motifs include flowers, medallions, leaves, shells, scrolls, and more.

Decorative Holdback

A **rosette**, above, is an **attractive solution for a holdback.** The colors in the finish pick up tones in the curtain's fabric.

Clean and Crisp

A **plain painted wood pole and finial,** opposite, keep this **youthful window treatment** simple and fresh.

Coordinated Look
The **gold-and-whitewashed finish on this finial,** above, picks up the **cream and gold tones** of the room.

A Dark Finish
Dark wood hardware, opposite top, provides a **handsome contrast** against the deep green walls and the **richly patterned floral drapery fabric.**

Sleek and Modern
Grommets, simple finials, and a **satin gold-tone finish,** opposite bottom, **enhance the modern tone** of the drapes for this contemporary living room.

designer hardware

The Right Mix
Wood finials, below, are an interesting contrast to the **wrought-iron poles** in this casual family room.

Classic Curl
The shape of this **wrought-iron holdback,** opposite, plays off the **paisley motif** in the **tone-on-tone fabric.**

Grand Illusion
Substantial hardware that is installed at the top of the wall makes simple double-hung windows look stately.

Pretty Informal

A **painted-blue pole and finial,** above, keep the feeling **casual and playful** in a young girl's room.

Added Interest

A **hammered-metal finial,** left, adds a handsome detail to these **textured sheer drapes.**

Strong Accent

A **metal holdback,** opposite, is a **great way to add embellishment** to a simple window treatment.

designer hardware

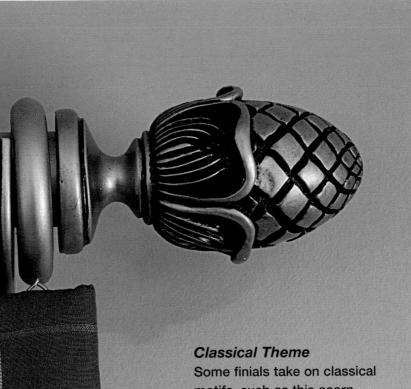

Classical Theme
Some finials take on classical motifs, such as this acorn. Here, an antique-gold finish adds extra glitz to the design.

details

It's easy to make curtain rings slide smoothly across a window—apply silicone spray to the top of the pole.

Creative Idea

A **decorative gilt bracket and finial,** opposite, adds punch to this
wood pole that has been **treated with a faux marble finish.**

Swank Style

This **cheetah's-head finial,** above, is a **wonderful accent piece** on
the **smartly dressed swags.** Animals, such as cats and rams, are often
the inspiration for a finial.

designer hardware

Pleasing Match
This pole and onion-style finial in a mahogany finish complements the strength of the crewel fabric nicely. The shiny brass bracket picks up the warm tones in the wood.

details

A bracket plays an important role in supporting rods and poles. If a treatment rubs against the window frame, an extension bracket solves the problem.

272

Part 2

window solutions

designs for difficult windows

If you're exasperated, here's a bevy of ideas for treating everything from an odd shape to an awkward location.

Sometimes windows are in locations that are difficult to treat. Or there may be one window that is out of place in terms of the size and style of other windows in the room.

There are many reasons why this may happen. Perhaps when the house was first built, its outside appearance took precedence over inside consistency. Or it has a new addition with windows that don't match the old ones. Or if old windows had to be replaced, local fire codes may have dictated a different size. Or an attic with dormer windows, originally intended for storage, has been transformed into an extra bedroom or a home office. In these situations, all it takes is a little bit of thought and imagination to come up with satisfying solutions.

details

A swag can have a deep or shallow drop. The deeper the drop, the fuller the folds. Jabots—the tails of fabric that complement swags—can be symmetrical or asymmetrical.

Architectural Cues

Today's **"architectural" windows** can be hard to dress, especially if you want to show off this handsome feature but still need to **control light and the view from outside.** Here, a **swag-and-jabot treatment** reveals the windows' pleasing lines, while **semisheer café curtains** filter sunlight and provide some privacy.

Odd Windows

Proportion is a design element that is important to all the components of a room. When a window is too tall, too narrow, too wide, or too short, it throws off the room's entire design. Fortunately, window treatments are a fabulous way to camouflage any of these flaws without the expense and upheaval of replacing the offending window.

Tall and Narrow. Though tall windows are desirable in most cases, certain styles can run too high and appear too narrow, adding an unwanted element to your room's design. For windows that are too tall, use a cornice or a valance to visually lower the length of the opening. If your window is too narrow, extend the curtains past the window frame, covering some of the wall. With shades or blinds, choose an outside mount to make the window seem wider.

details

When it comes to windows, matching style counts more than matching size or shape. When you're replacing a window, choose the same type as the existing ones. For example, don't install a casement window in a room (or even a house) with existing double-hung units.

Short and Wide. Some rooms call for dramatic windows. For instance, a formal dining room may have a group of small sash windows that seem insignificant in the scheme. To visually enlarge them, run a valance or cornice above the top of the window, and extend the curtains past the window frame. For an individual window that looks too short, try the same trick— place the curtain rod high on the wall, and hang floor-length panels. Even if you are using tabbed curtains rather than a formal arrangement, the two long curtain panels draw the eye upward, offsetting the short window. If the rod is visible, make sure the hardware is attractive or the finish ties in with the decor. Wide windows require different measures. To visually reduce the width, consider a floor-length curtain in a color that matches the walls to play down the horizontal form. Position the curtain so that it covers part of the window. Or consider a series of Roman or cascade shades to break up the horizontal line; the effect is increased if you adjust each shade to a different level.

MISMATCHED WINDOWS

Mismatched windows in a room are windows unlike each other in size or shape and lack any distinctive features that distinguish them as an architectural focal point. The goal is to make these windows appear as similar as possible.

Mismatched Sizes. If the size difference is not too great, install a valance or

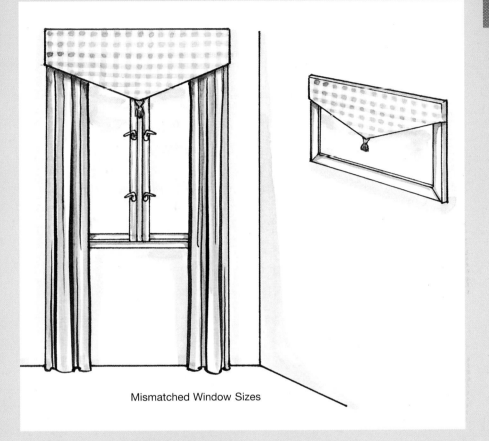

Mismatched Window Sizes

cornice above all of the windows at the same height. This may mean mounting a heading on the wall above a window. Use an outside mount to disguise the position of the frames. Mount shades or blinds directly under the header. If there is a big difference, plan the larger window first, and then scale the treatment down for the smaller window.

Mismatched Shapes. You can choose a different treatment for each window shape, but use the same fabrics. Link them by using the same hardware.

DIFFICULT LOCATIONS

Sometimes a window is situated in such a way that there is little room above or to the sides of the frame, or the window may be in a hard-to-get-at spot—a skylight, for example. Despite the location, aesthetics, privacy, or light control may necessitate some type of coverage.

Window Close to a Corner. When one of two windows is too close to a corner, choose a treatment that doesn't have to stack back. Blinds with a swag offer a functional yet decorative approach. Other ideas include café curtains with simple valances or sill-length tab curtains mounted inside the window frame. For a single window, consider emphasizing the asymmetry with a curtain that is tied back to one side.

Window Close to the Ceiling. If there isn't enough wall space for rod or track hardware, use ceiling hardware, or mount a lath onto the ceiling to support the rod or track, and cover it with a cornice. If you choose ceiling hardware, remember that the curtains will be stationary. Keep the style simple and the fabric lightweight because the hardware won't withstand heavier treatments. Or consider a cornice, which blocks the top of the window, helping to visually lower it.

Skylights. Most skylights are installed to increase light, so they are rarely covered. Sometimes, however, light is too glaring or makes the space too warm. A cellular shade with sidetracks to hold it flush against the window is a good solution, especially for insulation. If the shade is easily reached, it can be moved by

odd windows

hand. Otherwise, a telescoping pole or electronic control is required.

A casual solution, which uses woven blinds, works best where there is a series of skylights, such as in a garden room. Mount the blind at the top of the skylight. Run cording down both sides of the skylight and through rings that have been attached to each end of the blind's hem. When lowered, the blind bows gently in the center, so leave enough above-head clearance.

Skylight with
Cellular Shade

MORE CHALLENGES

Some windows present their own particular challenges because of their style or shape. The following pages explore solutions for many of these situations.

Tight Squeeze

One window is too close to a corner, opposite, in this cozy living room. Simple window coverings—**café curtains and swags without jabots**—downplay the problem.

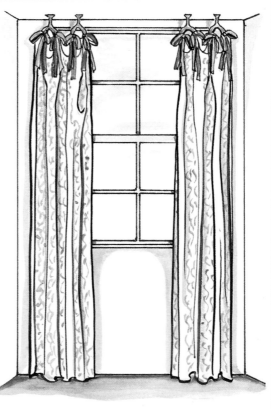

Window Close to Ceiling

Large Windows

Today, many homes feature a large window, such as a cathedral or geometric window, or several windows grouped together, such as a bay or Palladian window, dominating a wall. These windows are often an integral part of the architectural design of a room, providing access to beautiful views and allowing the maximum amount of light. In such cases, large or grouped windows are left untreated or framed with a swag. More often, however, the placement of these windows means that neighbors can see in and that the light can be overpowering during certain times of the day. To find the best treatment for these openings, consider the following ideas.

Cathedral or Palladian Windows. A wall of windows is a common feature in a modern room, and one that can be daunting to treat. If lack of privacy is the problem, treat the lower half of a large window with curtains on a traverse or curtain rod and leave the transoms unadorned. Vertical blinds are another option, but they may look too severe for your decor. Try topping the blinds with a swag or a valance to soften the effect. Both of these arrangements show off the shape of a window, while providing seclusion when needed.

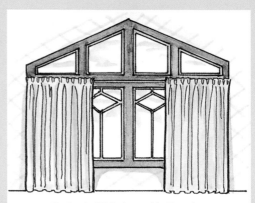

Cathedral Window with Curtains

Palladian Window with Scarf

Angled Window with Shirred Curtain

Glare from the rising or setting sun can make a room uncomfortable. If harsh light comes through the transoms, you can completely cover the window with drapery. Keep in mind that treating the window in this way may overwhelm the room and look too staged. Another option is to hang a scarf across the transom, which often blocks enough light to make the room comfortable again and is less obtrusive. You can also treat each transom individually. Try shirred curtains anchored at the top and bottom of the window by rods, or vertical blinds and cellular shades in specialty shapes. A valance in a simple style, such as a chevron, can be hung on each transom. Remember, if the top half of a window is covered, usually the bottom half should also be treated to balance out the arrangement.

Bay or Bow Windows. When dealing with bay or bow windows, first decide how you want to treat them: individually or as a group. For individual treatments, try matching shades, blinds, or shutters, which create a clean, modern look. Or add tieback curtains for a softer style. A bow window requires a curved rod, which requires professional installation, or a wire hanging system. Instead of hanging curtains directly on the window frame, consider mounting the rod on the wall above the bow or bay.

details

Install Roman shades on the individual units in a bay window. This versatile contemporary treatment will allow you to control light and privacy exactly where you need it.

Bay Windows with
Curtains and Valances

Bay Windows with
Curtains Outside of Recess

Special Shapes

Windows with special shapes, such as ovals, ellipses, triangles, and arches, usually exist because they add architectural interest, both inside and outside of the house. Sometimes the best solution is no treatment at all. If you like the look of a bare window but sun glare is a problem, investigate professionally applied window film. This transparent covering filters out the majority of the sun's damaging ultraviolet rays while minimally darkening the glass.

Circles and Ovals. For complete coverage, stationary cellular shades are available in custom shapes. If privacy isn't an issue, a scarf swag draped over a pole or through sconces is a pleasing choice because the curve of the scarf echoes the curve of the window.

Half-Rounds and Ellipses. Half-round and elliptical windows can be covered by a sunburst curtain, which is a rod-pocket curtain shirred on an arched rod. The lower edge is gathered into a rosette. Consider custom shutters and cellular shades, too.

Lancets. These Gothic-style arches can be difficult to treat. Try installing a shaped cornice with flanking curtains or

Scarf Swag on
a Circular Window

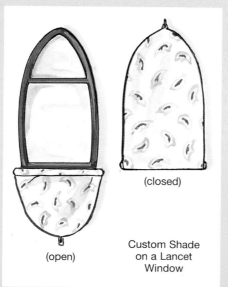

(closed)

(open)

Custom Shade
on a Lancet
Window

Shaped Cornice on a Lancet Window

specialty-shaped cellular shade. A bottom-hung shade with a shaped hem is a custom item that provides maximum privacy. The shade is pulled up and attached by a tab to a peg or a hook.

Triangular Windows. Most triangular windows are left unadorned because they are usually placed above another window. However, strong sunlight can be a problem. Because of the angled shape, rod-pocket curtains are one of the few styles that work. Custom shutters, cellular shades, and vertical blinds are also attractive solutions. Remember that some of these treatments are stationary.

Arched Windows. You can either include or ignore the arch. If you leave it untreated, you can hang any curtain, swag, valance, shade, or blind on the lower portion of the window. Simply run the top of the treatment under the bottom of the arch. To cover the arch, try a floor-length scarf that is gathered and secured around the curve. Or install a sunburst curtain on the arch with shirred panels below. The headings of festoon shades can be shaped to fit, too.

Shutters on an Elliptical Window

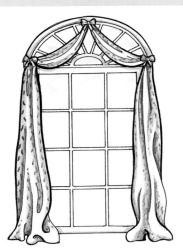

Scarf Swag on an Arched Window

Sunburst Curtain on a Half-Round Window

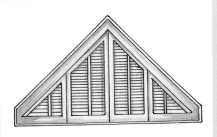

Shutters on a Triangular Window

Glazed Doors

No matter what type of glazed doors you have—French doors, sliding glass doors, or door-window combinations—the primary concern is leaving a clear passageway through the opening. If there is little wall space on either side of the opening, don't use a heavy fabric or a gathered curtain with a lot of fullness because it is too bulky and blocks access. Instead, choose a medium or light-weight fabric that stacks back tightly. If you are using a swag, check that it doesn't drape too low across the top where it can get caught in the door, particularly in the tracks of sliding glass doors.

Consider, too, which direction a door

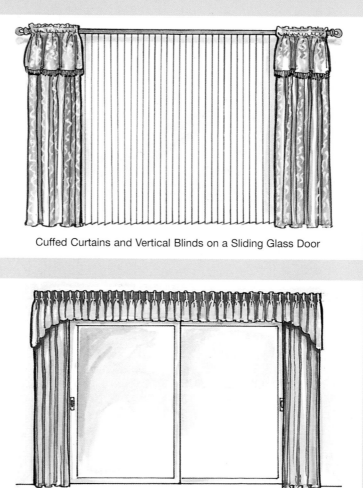

Cuffed Curtains and Vertical Blinds on a Sliding Glass Door

Valance and Curtains on a Sliding Glass Door

opens—in or out. There are more design options for an outward-opening door because a curtain is less likely to get caught in or block the door's operation. An inward-opening door often poses a problem; many curtain arrangements interfere with the movement of the door. Use treatments that can be secured above and below the glass on the door, such as some styles of shades, blinds, or shirred curtains on a pair of rods.

Sliding Glass Doors. Treatments that draw to one side, such as vertical blinds or curtains on a traverse rod, are the best options. Avoid any treatment that is mounted on the door itself because it will interfere with its operation.

French Doors. If the door opens out, a valance or cornice can be mounted at the top of the frame. If the door opens in, these headers are a possibility only if there is enough room to mount them on the wall above the door. Treatments that can be secured directly above and below the glass, and curtains that stack back tightly, work well. Shutters on tracks are a lovely choice, but they require substantial stack-back space.

Door-Window Combinations. You can treat this situation as one large unit, using the same guidelines as for sliding glass doors. For example, a valance or a cornice can unify the door and windows. Or you can dress each section individually with a series of matching elements. Try blinds on tracks or shades in tailored styles, such as roll-up or Roman ones.

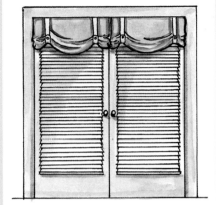

Blinds and Valance on French Doors

Shades on Windows and a Door

Curtains on French Doors

glazed doors

Dormer Windows

With dormer windows, you have the option of treating the window itself or the area outside of the recess—or both. Swing-out poles work best for hanging curtains on dormer windows because when light is needed, the poles swivel so that the curtain is against the wall. Use a lightweight fabric so that the hardware isn't overloaded. If there is enough clearance, consider a roller shade. For a dormer with a sloped ceiling, such as in an attic, here is a theatrical solution: hang a curtain rod on the wall outside of the recess; secure the curtain with a second rod placed at the point where the ceiling and the wall meet.

Hang It High

For a dormer, a valance and curtain are placed before the recess, creating a mock headboard above the bed.

Smocked Curtains with Two Rods

Rod-Pocket Curtains
on Swivel Rods

Corner Windows

When dressing corner windows, unify them with matching fabrics or a treatment that visually joins the two windows together. Pull them together with a valance or a cornice—both treatments turn corners neatly. Curtains are also a good way to connect the windows. There is also a variety of tieback options. The panels can be tied back-to-back, or they can mirror each other. Formal window dressings involve a combination of both styles. Try balloon or cloud shades, too. Have the shade extend past the window slightly so that the corner is visually filled in; the fullness of the treatment helps to cover any gaps. Swags and jabots also bridge the gap. Cascade tails, in particular, visually complement each other in a corner.

Swags and Jabots with
Tied-Back Curtains

Curtains in
"Mirror" Arrangement

Balloon Shades

dormer and corner windows

appendix

Measuring Your Windows

The first step, in order to ensure that your chosen window treatment is a success, is to take a complete set of measurements for each window. The illustration opposite shows the parts of a standard double-hung window, which you should refer to as you read the instructions that follow for measuring for treatments requiring hardware mounted both outside and inside the window opening. Follow these three suggestions for greater accuracy: use a sturdy, retractable metal measuring tape; ask someone to assist you; and use a stepladder to get the higher measurements. Be sure to double-check your figures.

INSIDE MOUNT

For a window treatment that you want to install inside the window opening, there are a few simple measurements to take: the length of the window from the top of the frame to the sill, and the inside width of the window. Because some windows are not perfectly plumb, take these measurements in three spots, and then working with the narrowest measurement, round up to the nearest $\frac{1}{8}$ inch. Do this for both the width and the length. Although this type of installation is more common for shades, blinds, or shutters, occasionally it is used for a curtain.

OUTSIDE MOUNT

Curtains, more often than shades, blinds, and shutters, are typically installed as an outside mount. Hardware, such as rods, poles, and brackets, are attached to the trim or wall outside the window opening. Decide where you want to install the curtain rod, and then measure the width from bracket to bracket. Add at least 3 inches to allow a center overlap. (If you are using a curved rod, add twice the number of inches the rod projects from the wall.)

Next, decide where you want the bottom of the curtain to fall: at the sill, the apron, or the floor; then measure down to that spot from the bottom of the rod, pole, or bracket. (If the curtain will hang from rings, measure from the base of the rings once they are installed on the rod or bracket.) Allow an extra 2 inches for hardware.

measure twice, cut once

Ensure success by starting your window treatment project with accurate measurements. You might even organize them in a notebook, adding photographs of styles you're considering, along with your favorite fabric swatches.

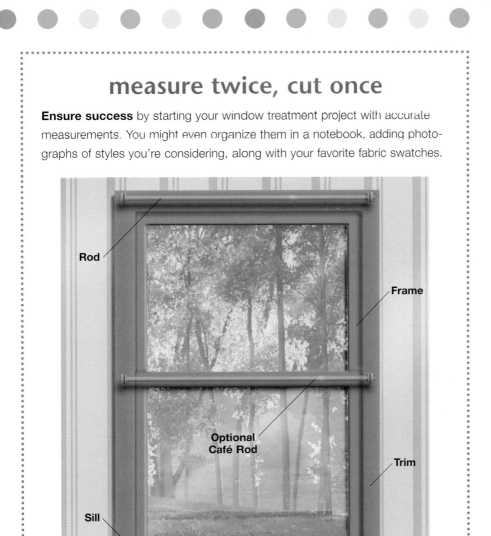

Rod

Frame

Optional
Café Rod

Trim

Sill

Apron

resources

The following list of manufacturers and associations is meant to be a general guide to additional industry and product-related sources. It is not intended as a listing of products and manufacturers represented by the photographs in this book.

American Society of Interior Designers, Inc. (ASID)
202-546-3480
www.asid.org
Provides consumers with information about interior-design subjects, including design programs and continuing education. Its Web site offers a designer referral service.

Atlas Homewares
818-240-3500
www.atlashomewares.com
Sells decorative hardware. Ideas for unique tiebacks are found on the Web site.

Brewster Wallcovering Co.
800-366-1700
www.brewp.com
Manufactures valances, borders, fabric, and wallpaper in a wide variety of styles and collections.

Calico Corners
800-213-6366
www.calicocorners.com
Sells decorator fabric. In-store services include design consultation and custom window-treatment fabrication.

Comfortex Window Fashions
800-843-4151
www.comfortex.com
Manufacturers custom window treatments. The product line includes sheer and pleated shades, wood shutters, and blinds.

Country Curtains
800-456-0321
www.countrycurtains.com
Sells ready-made curtains, shades, blinds, hardware, and accessories, in-store and on-line.

Eisenhart Wallcoverings Company
800-726-3267
Manufactures coordinated wallcoverings and fabrics.

F. Schumacher & Co.
800-523-1200
www.fschumacher.com
Manufactures coordinated wallcoverings and fabrics.

Graber Window Fashions
Spring Industries
800-221-6352
www.springs.com
Manufactures shades, blinds, and window hardware.

Hancock Fabrics
877-322-7427
www.hancockfabrics.com
Sells fabric and trimmings.

Hunter Douglas, Inc.
800-789-0331
www.hunterdouglas.com
Manufactures shades, blinds, and shutters.
Its Web site directs consumers to designers,
dealers, and installers.

Kirsch Window Fashions
800-817-6344
www.kirsch.com
Manufactures blinds, rods, shades, and
holdbacks.

Levolor
800-538-6567
www.levolor.com
Manufactures a variety of blinds, including
vertical, wood, and cordless types, as well
as cellular shades.

Portsmouth Drapery Hardware Co.
603-373-8457
www.draperyhardware.com
Manufactures fabrics and easy-to-install
window hardware for residential and
commercial use.

Scalamandré
800-932-4361
www.scalamandre.com
Manufactures and imports high-end fabrics and
trimmings for the professional interior-design
trade.

Seabrook Wallcoverings
901-320-3611
www.seabrookwallcoverings.com
Manufactures and distributes coordinated
wallcoverings and fabrics.

Smith & Noble
800-248-8888
www.smithandnoble.com
Catalog source for ready-made and custom
window treatments, fabric, and hardware.

Spiegel
800-222-5680
www.spiegel.com
Catalog source for window treatments,
hardware, and related embellishments.

Springs Industries, Inc.
888-926-7888
www.springs.com
Manufactures window treatments, including
blinds and shutters.

Thibaut Wallcoverings
800-223-0704
www.thibautdesign.com
Manufactures coordinated wallcoverings and
fabrics.

Waverly
800-423-5881
www.waverly.com
Manufacturers coordinated wallcoverings and
fabrics, as well as ready-made curtains and
accessories.

**Window Coverings of America Association
(WCAA)**
888-298-9222
www.wcaa.org
A nonprofit trade organization that represents
the window-coverings industry.

glossary

Austrian Shade A fabric shade that falls in cascading scallops and is operated with a cord.

Awning Window A hinged, horizontal window that opens outward and is often operated with a crank system.

Balloon Shade A fabric shade that falls in full blousy folds at the bottom and is operated with a cord.

Bay Window A multiple-window unit projecting out from the exterior wall of a house, forming an angled recess inside the house.

Bow Window A large window that is similar to a bay unit, but the recess is curved.

Box Pleats Two folds turned toward each other, creating a flat-fronted pleat.

Brackets Hardware attached to the window to support the curtain rod or pole.

Brocade A weighty, typically formal fabric in silk, cotton, or wool. It is distinguished by a raised, often floral, design in a jacquard weave.

Buckram A coarse fabric, stiffened with glue, that is used to give body and shape to curtain headings.

Cased Heading Fabric folded over and anchored with a row of stitches to form a rod pocket.

Casement Window A hinged vertical window that opens in or out and is often operated with a crank mechanism.

Chintz A cotton fabric that is coated with a resin to give it a sheen.

Clerestory Window A window set near the ceiling.

Cloud Shade A balloon shade that has a gathered or pleated heading and is operated with a cord.

Cornice A projecting, decorative box that is installed above a window.

Damask A jacquard-weave fabric made of cotton, silk, wool, or a combination with a satin, raised design. Widely used for draperies.

Dormer Window A window set into the front face of a dormer.

Double-Hung Window The most common type, consisting of two sash, one atop the other, which slide up and down to open and close the window.

Draping A technique of folding, looping, and securing fabric in graceful folds and

curves. The drape of a curtain is the way it hangs.

Face Fabric The primary, outer fabric used in a window treatment.

Finial The decorative ends of a curtain rod or pole.

Flemish Heading A pleat that is stuffed with batting for a puffed appearance; also called a "goblet pleat."

Festoon Shade A shade that is made of gathered fabric, such as an Austrian, balloon, or cloud shade.

French Door A door, typically with 12 divided panes of glass, used alone or in pairs. It is also used as a fixed window.

Goblet Pleat See Flemish Heading.

Heading The horizontal area at the top of a curtain. Its style determines how a curtain hangs.

Holdback Curtain hardware made of metal, wood, or glass. It is installed into the wall or on the window trim and is used in place of a tieback.

Interlining Made of lightweight, opaque fabric, a layer between the curtain fabric and the lining that adds body and blocks light.

Jabot The vertical element that hangs at the side of a sweeping scallop (swag) or crescent-shape drape of fabric at the top of a window.

Jacquard A loom, named after its inventor, that uses punched cards to weave intricate raised designs. Brocade and damask are jacquard fabrics.

Lambrequin A painted board or stiffened fabric that surrounds the top and side of a window or a door. Historically, it also was drapery that hung from a shelf, such as a mantel.

Lining An underlayer of fabric that is added to a curtain for extra body and to filter light and air.

Miter A sewing technique for creating a flat corner where two hemmed edges of fabric meet.

Moiré A fabric finish on silk or acetate, intended to resemble water marking.

Muslin A plain-weave cotton; also called "voile."

Pattern Matching To align a repeating pattern when joining together two pieces of fabric.

Piping An edging made of cording encased in bias-cut fabric.

Pleater Hooks Metal hooks that are inserted into pleating tape to create pleats in a curtain heading.

Pleating Tape A cotton or nylon strip, with drawstrings, that is sewn onto the back of the heading to make pleats.

Roller Shade A fabric or vinyl shade that is attached to a spring-loaded roller.

Roman Shade A fabric shade that falls into flat, horizontal folds. It is raised by a cord system.

Stack-Back The space along the sides of a window taken up by a curtain when it is drawn back.

Swag A sweeping scallop or crescent-shape drape of fabric at the top of a window. In a swag-and-jabot treatment, it is the center element that is flanked by one or a set of tails (jabots).

Taffeta A silk-and-acetate weave that appears shiny and maintains shape. It is used for formal-style curtains, draperies, and shades.

Tail See Jabot.

Tieback A fabric strip or cord used to hold curtains open; also a style of curtain.

Toile de Jouy An eighteenth-century design of pastoral, allegorical, or romantic scenes printed in one color on cotton or linen. It is named for the French town, Jouy, where it orginated. Today, toile is reproduced in numerous colors and on various fabrics.

Traverse Rod A rod from which curtains are hung that features a track system or runners.

Valance A short length of fabric that hangs along the top of a window, with or without a curtain underneath.

Voile See Muslin.

index

photo credits

All "before" shots, illustrations, and designs by Nancee Brown, ASID unless otherwise noted. All photos by Melabee M Miller unless otherwise noted.

page 1: design: Judy Collins **page 3:** design: Pat Mills, Byford & Mills **page 9:** *top right* design: Greta Goss, Greta Goss, LLC *bottom right* design: Jo Ann Alston, Allied Member ASID, J. Stephens Interiors **page 11:** Andrew Yaniuk *bottom* Nancee Brown **page 18:** design: Anne Goldsmith, Anne Goldsmith Interiors **page 19:** design: Jo Ann Alston, Allied Member ASID, J. Stephens Interiors **page 20:** Andrew Yaniuk **page 21:** Nancee Brown **page 22-3:** Bill Rothschild **page 24:** Bob Allen Associates **page 25:** Bill Rothschild **page 26:** courtesy of Graber **page 28:** design: Elizabeth Gillin, Elizabeth Gillin Interiors **page 30:** design: Jo Ann Alston, Allied Member ASID, J. Stephens Interiors **page 31:** design: Michelle Koenig, Bruchele Interiors **page 32:** design: Maryann Pennella **page 33:** Andrew Yaniuk **page 34:** design: Claudia Panizza, CP Design **page 35:** design: Jeffrey Queripel, Queripel Interiors **pages 36-37:** Nancee Brown **page 38:** design: Rosalie Stolinski, Interiors by Rosalie **page 39:** Bill Rothschild **page 44:** Nancee Brown **page 45:** design: Karen Luongo, AIA, Kapuscinski * Luongo Architects **page 47:** design: Greta Goss, Greta Goss, LLC **page 48:** design: Beth Insabella Walsh IIDA, ASID, Insabella Design **page 49:** design: Greta Goss, Greta Goss, LLC **page 50:** design: Geri Ruka, Geri Ruka Assoc., Inc. **page 51:** Nancee Brown **page 57:** *bottom left* design: Tammy Kaplan, Images in Design **page 58:** Jessie Walker, design: unknown **page 59:** Eric Roth **page 63:** design: Suzanne Curtis, ASID, Suzanne Curtis Interior Design **page 64:** design: Christine Thompson, Grapevine Interiors, LLC **page 65:** design: Laurie Fritze, ASID, Oakleigh Interiors **page 66:** design: Lisa Melone **page 67:** design: Elizabeth Gillin, Elizabeth Gillin

Interiors **page 71:** design: Susan Rosenthal & Rosemarie Cicio IF, Susan Rosenthal, IIDA, ASID **pages 72-73:** design: Jennifer Pacca, Award Interiors **page 74:** Andrew Yaniuk **page 75:** design: Susan Rosenthal, Susan Rosenthal IIDA, LLC **page 78:** design: Elizabeth Gillin, Elizabeth Gillin Interiors **page 79:** design: Judy Collins **page 84:** design: Rosalie Stolinski, Interiors by Rosalie **page 85:** design: Barbara Noud, Allied Member ASID, Lifestyle Interiors **page 86:** Andrew Yaniuk **page 87:** design: Arlene Reilly, Bernards Decorating Inc. **pages 88-89:** design: Modeste A. Sobolta, AIA, Elkin Sobolta **page 90:** design: Barbara Noud, Allied Member ASID, Lifestyle Interiors **page 91:** design: Suzanne Curtis, ASID, Suzanne Curtis Interior Design **page 92:** design: Jennifer Pacca, Award Interiors **page 93:** design: Laurie Fritze, ASID, Oakleigh Interiors **page 94-96:** design: Arlene Reilly, Bernards Decorating Inc. **page 97:** design: Jennifer Pacca, Award Interiors **page 98:** Nancee Brown **page 99:** design: Jennifer Pacca, Award Interiors **page 101:** Michael Jones *bottom right* Nicholas Brown **page 102:** design: Ellen Brownstein, The Classy Casa, LLC **page 105:** design: James Greener, AIA & Judy Mashburn, James Greener, AIA/CTS Group **pages 106-107:** design: Don Kossar & Ellen Fawer, Kossar Fawer **page 108:** design: Greta Goss, Greta Goss, LLC **page 110:** design: Jeffrey Queripel, Queripel Interiors **pages 112-113:** design: Marlene Wangenheim, Interiors by Design, Inc. **page 114:** design: James Greener, AIA & Judy Mashburn, James Greener, AIA/CTS Group **page 115:** design: Jennifer Pacca, Award Interiors **page 116:** design: Arthur Simon & Mary Ann Imbriaco, Designs for Interiors **page 117:** no design credit **page 120:** design: Lawrence-Mayer-Wilson **page 123:** design: Diane Romanowski & Suzette Donleavy, Diane Romanowski Interior Design & Well-Designed Interiors **page 125:** design: Pat Mills, Byford & Mills **page 126:** design: Marlene Wangenheim,

Have a home improvement, decorating, or gardening project?

Look for these and other fine

Creative Homeowner books

wherever books are sold.

300 color photos. 304 pp.; 7" × 9¼"
$19.95 (US) $21.95 (CAN)
BOOK #: 279659

300 color photos. 304 pp.; 7" × 9¼"
$19.95 (US) $21.95 (CAN)
BOOK #: 279648

300 color photos. 304 pp.; 7" × 9¼"
$19.95 (US) $21.95 (CAN)
BOOK #: 279082

400 color photos. 304 pp.; 9¼"×10⅞"
$24.95 (US) $29.95 (CAN)
BOOK #: 279679

For more information and to order directly, go to
www.creativehomeowner.com